Healing

MY PILGRIMAGE WITH TAGORE, INDIA'S REVERED TEACHER

Linda L. George, Ph.D.

Gotham Books
30 N Gould St.
Ste. 20820, Sheridan, WY 82801
https://gothambooksinc.com/
Phone: 1 (307) 464-7800

© 2022 Linda L. George, Ph.D.. All rights reserved.

No part of this book may be reproduced, stored in a retrieval system, or transmitted by any means without the written permission of the author.

Published by Gotham Books (August 9, 2022)

ISBN: 979-8-88775-030-9 (h)
ISBN: 979-8-88775-002-6 (sc)
ISBN: 979-8-88775-003-3 (e)

Any people depicted in stock imagery provided by iStock are models, and such images are being used for illustrative purposes only.

certain stock imagery © iStock.

Because of the dynamic nature of the Internet, any web addresses or links contained in this book may have changed since publication and may no longer be valid. The views expressed in this work are solely those of the author and do not necessarily reflect the views of the publisher, and the publisher hereby disclaims any responsibility for them.

Contents

Dedication 5
Pacific Book Review 7
The Journey Begins 9
The Rishi, The Rabbi, and Me 12
Three Marriages 16
Whatever Is Lost, Stolen, Or Dies 22
Tagore And Gandhi 23
God's Fault? 25
Too Reserved For The World 31
Song And Dance 35
"Wolf Sister" 38
Hope In The Darkness 40
Patriotism That Isolates 45
Grief is Messy 49
Don't Give Up 53
Proving My Worth 60
Gifts Offered, But Rejected 64
Following My Own Path 70
Prayer Time 73
The Weaker Sex? 78
Unsung Song 83
The Impossible Dream 88
Mother And Daughter 93
Getting To Know You 96
Poop, Poverty, And Plague 99
The Power Of One 103
Castes 106
Forgiveness 110

Hold My Hand	114
Many Worlds	120
Burying One's Child	131
Seeing God	134
Searching For Home	139
Lessons From Tagore On Healing	143
The Journey Continues	151
References	155

Dedication

To my sisters Sharon and Debra, who have always been there for me.

Pacific Book Review

This moving memoir tells the story of two people's lives: author Linda George and renowned Indian poet Rabindranath Tagore. *Healing; My Pilgrimage with Tagore, India's Revered Teacher* will enlighten and engage readers.

George's eloquent writing is so emotional and heartfelt that readers will instantly connect with *Healing: My Pilgrimage with Tagore, India's Revered Teacher.* The book would be ideal for readers who are on a spiritual journey. Even for readers who are not, they can appreciate the lessons about love and gratitude and how to overcome difficult life challenges.

US Review of Books

Author Linda George "writes with tenderness and solemnity about the losses we all must experience . . . Relating her personal burdens and uplifting moments to Tagore's poetic vision allows her readers to share a sense of reverence and the abiding hopefulness of an all-encompassing view of life."

Reviewed by: Barbara Bamberger Scott

The Journey Begins

Did you ever have a favorite toy, or car, or piece of jewelry, or something else you treasured that broke? It feels like the whole world is broken: broken dreams, broken hearts, broken lives, broken planet. Unless it's happening in our own families or neighborhoods, we often try to look the other way and hope someone else will fix it. Then something terrible and frightening happens to me or to you, and we sit up and pay attention. And we cry out for help.

All of us who are over five years old will likely retain for the rest of our lives the fear and pain that began in 2020 when COVID-19 emerged. This worldwide pandemic strikes mercilessly in every location where humans reside. Unimaginable numbers of people are suffering and dying while often isolated from their loved ones. Countless others will survive this brutal assault, but with debilitating side effects for many years, perhaps for the rest of their lives. One medical professional I know, who has worked nonstop for months in a COVID-19 intensive care unit, said that what may be even worse for her than not being able to save her patients is seeing the scans of what is going on inside the bodies of those who survive. She says it's terrifying.

Millions more who may escape sickness or death are suffering profound effects financially, emotionally, and psychologically. These include loss of jobs, homes, businesses, and loved ones. Other challenges include social isolation, social anxiety, food insecurity, inability to purchase medications, educational sacrifices, and domestic violence. Additionally, our precious Earth is suffering because of climate instability. Feelings of helplessness and hopelessness are contributing to increasing levels of depression and suicide. All these events mirror the countless ways we experience suffering and loss. It reminds us of our limitations, our anguish, and our deepest fears.

These are topics we tend to shy away from because they are too difficult, too personal, too emotional. Many societal influences encourage us to minimize or ignore those fragile places in our lives and souls.

Almost every adult, and many young people, can mark at least one specific day on the calendar that signifies a grief-related occurrence: the death of a loved one, a divorce or breakup, a debilitating accident, a frightening diagnosis, or a devastating betrayal. And on and on. Two dates in my life that screamed help for many years are May 8, 1993, and July 25, 2014, but I'm getting ahead of myself.

I decided, after much thought and prayer, that it was time for me to dust off some extensive work I did about healing, and how the teachings and life experiences of a man from a different culture and time helped me find wholeness.

Several years ago, I heard someone recite a poem that spoke to the depths of my soul. I found out that the poem was by Rabindranath Tagore, a person whose name was completely unfamiliar to me. I located the poem, and I was hooked on Tagore, even though I knew nothing about him at that point. As soon as I knew how to spell his name, I started doing informal research to find some more of his poetry and to learn a bit about him. I never dreamed that my initial, informal, introduction to Tagore would become my life's passion.

My astonishment about Tagore continued to grow as I discovered the massive influence of this man's life, and the encyclopedic amount of material that he authored. It only takes a couple of internet searches to discover hundreds of books and articles written about him in English; the quantity of works about him in other languages easily doubles the total.

How is it, I wondered, that I had successfully navigated many years of formal, advanced education, yet I had never heard of Rabindranath Tagore? His beloved home was India, though he traveled all over the world well before most people went further than the boundaries of their own state or province. He was born in 1861 and lived to the age of eighty, an unbelievably long life for that time.

One of the facts I learned early on about Tagore related to how many of his close loved ones died; several of them within the span of a few years, before Tagore reached the age of forty-five. I felt amazed and astonished that, in the midst of so much personal devastation and grief, Tagore continued his massive output of writings and songs.

As a professional clergyperson, I have counseled thousands of grieving individuals. Many of them expect nothing from me except a compassionate response. Many of them come to me trying to resolve feelings of guilt, of anger, and of fear. Many of them want help as they try to make some sense of a senseless situation. And all of them hope that I can help them find some spiritual solace. I always try to remain sensitive to what a humbling and sobering responsibility it is to hold someone's bleeding heart in my hands. Although Tagore and I come from different ethnic, cultural, and spiritual backgrounds, I recognized in his writings a kindred spirit and a fount of wisdom and healing.

Sometimes, persons who attempt to offer solace to another unintentionally cause the bereaved one to feel worse. It is not easy to know why one person's outreach is comforting and another's is not. From the beginning of my relationship with Tagore, I sensed that his poetry and essays reflect a life complicated and enriched by the height and depth of emotions. It wasn't his scholarship or keen intellect or immense curiosity about life that drew me to him; it was his heart. I knew his had been broken, too.

The Rishi, The Rabbi, and Me

Rabindranath Tagore was born into a highly regarded and privileged family in the middle of the 19th century. Nineteen centuries earlier, my first spiritual guide, Jesus, was born out of wedlock to a child-woman with no material or social status. The child from India grew up hating traditional school, but loving the study of the sciences, mathematics, history, literature, music, and several languages. The other boy received little or no formal schooling, but he learned how to build a house, and a boat, and a yoke for the oxen. Both suckled on stories from their respective heritages and learned how to weave a tale for the mind and the soul.

I only met Tagore, the rishi, in my late forties when someone recited a poem of the Indian's. My sense of Tagore's authenticity and depth tugged at my heart for several years until I believed that he was calling me into his heart.

I've loved Jesus, the rabbi, since before I was born. His teachings, and stories and songs about him, nurture my life every day. When I first suspected that he envisioned a special calling for me, I was about twelve or thirteen, the age of his mother Mary when she gave birth to him.

Rabindranath Tagore was an upper caste Indian from the Bengal province. He grew up in a sprawling mansion bursting with several generations of extended family members. His lifespan, from 1861 till 1941, almost exactly coincided with the British colonization of India. Grief and sadness punctuated his long life with alarming frequency.

No one could have imagined that the fame of this reclusive fourteenth child would eclipse that of his beloved and highly regarded father and grandfather.[1] When Tagore won the Nobel Prize for Literature in 1913, almost no one beyond the shores of India had ever heard of him.² When he arrived in Sweden to accept the prize, the beard framing his dark face, his floor-length white robes, and his piercing eyes caused people to turn and stare. Within a few years, his reputation worldwide equaled that of his dear friend Mohandas Gandhi.

Gandhi nicknamed Tagore "The Great Sentinel," because of his penetrating insights into the future of India and her relationship with the rest of the world.³ When Tagore died in 1941, at the age of 80, accolades and expressions of sympathy and grief poured into India like a deluge.⁴ And yet, many Americans of non-Indian heritage have never heard of Rabindranath Tagore.

Yeshua, known to most non-Jewish Westerners as Jesus, began life without the status of two parents who were married to each other. This fact, largely ignored or whitewashed for two millennia, must have been a decisive influence in shaping this child who would change the world. In a time and place when "traditional family values" dictated every aspect of daily life and society, an unwed mother and her come-lately husband would have struggled mightily to receive the warm embrace of their little community. Never in his entire life would the seed of that union be allowed to forget that he was only a bastard child from a poor family.⁵

Rabindranath and Jesus hailed from different ancient eastern traditions, centuries apart, and both of them alchemized painful life experiences into golden balm to soothe the world's hurts. Both were word-artists who loved God and stories and music. Both men adored children, and embraced the children's wisdom and innocence and openness. Both men traveled widely and observed life and nature with keen eyes and open minds. And both men understood that those times when life seems neither fair nor just do not reflect the heart of the Giver of life.

The pictures and stories of the bearded Jesus surrounded me from my birth. He is and always has been my friend and my guide to holiness. As I have become increasingly acquainted with the pictures and stories and poetry of the bearded Tagore, I also consider him my friend and a guide to holiness.

I find it impossible to embrace the spirituality exemplified by Tagore, without reference to Jesus whose Christly incarnation has colored my entire life. That is not to say that I demand of Tagore, or anyone else, a belief in Jesus as the Christ. Tagore was not a Christian, though he grew to understand and respect the values and teachings of Jesus. So many things Tagore said about spirituality and worship remind me of Jesus's teachings as I understand them. Tagore wrote, "I believe in a spiritual world – not as anything separate from this world – but as its innermost truth. With the breath we draw we must always feel this truth, that we are living in God."[6]

Jesus never required anyone to believe what he believed about God, or to share his religious heritage. Jesus offered healing to people whose wounds were visible and invisible. He offered healing to people whose hearts broke over mistreatment by their own families and communities, their own governments, and their own religious institutions.

Through poetry and music and drama and other creative endeavors, Tagore also offered healing to the broken-hearted and downtrodden, regardless of their ethnic or spiritual background. Both Jesus and Rabindranath lived and taught a spirituality that embraces people's differences and encourages them to acknowledge their own holiness and the holiness of others. Both men, whom I embrace as my teachers, saw the world through the lens of grief and helped transform their own grief and that of others into healing. Both men have taught me much about finding my way through grief, and about how I can embody compassion to others in their times of grief.

1. Kripalani, 2008, pp. 23–5
2. Kripalani, 2008, pp. 251–8
3. Dutta & Robinson, 2009, p.13
4. Dutta & Robinson, 2009, pp. 366–9
5. Chilton, 2002, pp. 13–17
6. Tagore, 2006, p. 140

Three Marriages

One of the most difficult periods of my life began on May 8, 1993, when two senior military officers in their dress uniforms showed up at my front door to tell me that my husband, Jerry, had died in a car accident that morning. Years earlier, I had traversed much of the landscape of grief during and following an abusive marriage. The pain at that time was intense, frightening, isolating, and seemed never-ending. After Jerry died, I descended into a depth of hell I never could have imagined.

August 2012 immersed me into another ocean of grief: Wayne, my beloved husband of eighteen years, received a diagnosis of esophageal cancer, one of the most aggressive forms of cancer. The first doctor suggested that the cancer might be recently developed, small, and easily removed, like a grape on a stalk. The cancer was deeply embedded and at least stage three. Months of tests, life-sucking procedures, nausea, weight loss, infirmity, and pain debilitated Wayne so much that we weren't sure he could endure the massive, necessary surgery. For many months, Wayne needed my help around the clock, and I am so grateful that my retirement status, my health, and our finances allowed me to devote myself to his care.

From my current perspective, I can honestly say that I would not change the events in my life. I am certain that I would not have pursued theological training and ordination to ministry if I had stayed married to my first husband. The grief I experienced during that marriage, and following my divorce, baptized me in the pool of grief. I was twenty-two years old and did not know anyone else who was divorced. I was relieved that nobody judged me in my new status; most people didn't seem to care. I felt so lonely and ashamed. I spent several years nurturing anger against him for how he treated me, but, more than that, I realized how much anger I internalized for letting myself be so degraded. In our society, feeling humiliated is seldom acknowledged as grief, and yet it surely tends the flames of countless acts of spousal abuse as well as all manner of suicides and homicides. I am truly thankful we ended that marriage before the acrimony devolved into something much worse. I am also exceedingly grateful that I found ways to learn about myself and honor myself so that I would not enter another abusive partnership.

When Jerry died, I was forty-two. At that time, I helped pastor a military congregation that included about 150 active retirees. I can't imagine what I would have done without them. Many of them were widowed, and all suffered with friends whose life mates had died. My friends and coworkers closer to my own age seemed afraid of being around me, as if they might catch widowhood. Since Jerry and I were both army chaplains, I think many of the younger folks became truly terrified about their own and their family's mortality. If this kind of tragedy could happen in a family with two clergy, then it could surely happen to anybody.

Since Wayne's illness, dear friends and family, and hundreds of people we don't even know, have carried us through. My own inner strength, my faith in God, and my empathy with others grew in proportion to the depths of my pain and the love I have experienced through my life thus far. The person I am today, the relationships I enjoy, and the visions I pursue for my life are directly related to how I have traversed through grief's byways.

As I read about Tagore—study his writings, music, and paintings,—I never cease to marvel that he created so much beauty and hope and wonderment out of so much pain in his life. When Rabindranath was only 14, his mother died. His young wife, three of their children, his beloved sister-in-law, and his father, all died by the time he was 45 years old.

In addition to the deaths of many beloved family members and friends, Tagore also suffered greatly because of the difficult situations in his homeland and around the world. Unlike most Indians of his generation, he traveled extensively—throughout India and the globe. He was a keen observer of nature and of people everywhere. He welcomed conversations with people of all occupations, socio-economic backgrounds, nationalities, and all ages. Although he was educated and from an upper caste, he never ceased trying to understand and to assist persons oppressed by poverty, illiteracy, and injustice.

Throughout my career as a clergyperson and counselor, and as part of my own healing, I have studied many books about grief. With rare exception, the focus of the treatises relates to the death or terminal illness of a loved one. I am not minimizing the depth and breadth of watching someone suffer or experiencing the death of a beloved. What interests me is that terminal illness and death almost seem to be the only grief stimuli our culture acknowledges. Other common causes of grief include divorce, death of a pet, moving, sickness, loss of employment, relationship challenges, and financial crises.

Tagore's grief surrounding the deaths of many dear loved ones punctuated his writings for his entire life. Perhaps, because he did not deny that pain, he allowed himself to mourn many other experiences in his life. The poet suffered the loss of his quiet, secluded lifestyle following his Nobel Prize and subsequent scrutiny. He suffered intensely because the school and university he founded were targets of ridicule and misunderstanding. When his beloved home, Bengal, endured years of Hindu-Muslim conflicts provoked by government interference, Tagore's writings and songs pleading for unity got lost in the din of fighting and resistance. The prevalent and long-standing practices of child marriage and widowed burning ripped through Tagore's soul. He grieved the entire anti-British movement led by Gandhi; the poet correctly predicted increasing violence, tearing apart his beloved India. Many other events anguished Tagore throughout his long life.

Rabindranath's poetry and songs enabled his own healing and offered hope and consolation to people around the world. They have offered me a fertile path for my own healing. I believe that other grief-weary people in the 21st century can likewise find solace through the wisdom of Tagore.

Some things I know for sure about grief are these:

First, intellectual knowledge about grief in no way correlates to actually experiencing grief.

Second, any specific grief response may have little relationship to the time when the grief stimulus occurred.

Third, people's responses to grief are totally subjective, often based on their life experiences up to that point.

Fourth, grief-work happens in uneven and unexpected layers; an event or memory that wedges open one's heart may seem completely unrelated to the original grief event.

Finally, though everyone's grief experiences are unique, telling our own stories, and listening to one another's stories, help us gain insights into healing.

I have been an ordained Christian clergyperson since 1981. I served in full-time ministry, as an institutional chaplain, as a hospital chaplain and as a United States Army chaplain, for thirty years. By choice, my entire ministerial career has been in ecumenical/interfaith settings. I believe that Tagore's faith in God guided his life and life-work. What initially drew me to Tagore were his writings about the spiritual life and his spiritual poetry.

> Accept me, dear God, accept me for this while.
> Let those orphaned days that passed without You be forgotten.
> Only spread this little moment wide across Your lap, holding it under Your light.
> I have wandered in pursuit of voices that drew me, yet led me nowhere.
> Now let me sit in peace and listen to Your words in the soul of my silence.
> Do not turn away Your face from my heart's dark secrets, but burn them till they are alight with Your fire.
>
> —Tagore [7]

A challenge that I struggled with throughout my career in the army, and continuing, is the opinion espoused by many Christians that the only way to God is through Jesus. One of the things I treasure most about my army career is the relationships I developed with persons from numerous spiritual traditions. It is unlikely that I would have been blessed by so many friendships with Jews, Muslims, Wiccans, Bahais, and Christians from the full spectrum of Protestantism, Orthodoxy, and Roman Catholicism, had I chosen a path of traditional ministry in local congregations. The belief that all people are spiritual beings guides my life, and that how we address God or practice our spiritual traditions should be a unifying factor, not a divisive factor. Throughout most of Tagore's life, he cherished meeting and learning from persons of all spiritual backgrounds. The ancient Hindu scripture that he culled to model his university speaks not only of academic outreach, but of embracing all as the family of God: "…where the world makes its home in a single nest" [8]

[7] Tagore, 1997b, p. 1
[8] Das Gupta, 2004, pp. 30–1

Whatever Is Lost, Stolen, Or Dies

Several years ago, after the death of my former husband Jerry, I found among his papers, in his own handwriting, a formula that is the best definition of grief I have ever read. He and I had never talked about this, and despite searching for the source of that definition, I have been unable to locate it anywhere. I, therefore, believe that Jerry Ambler authored it. **"Grief is whenever anyone or anything that you love, cherish, or prize, is lost, stolen, or dies."** Clearly, this definition encompasses a far broader understanding of grief than the death of a loved one.

Let us consider a few common examples of grief-inducing experiences: Your house is burglarized or destroyed by fire, water, or storm; a precious memento is lost or stolen; a beloved pet becomes seriously ill and dies; the woods and stream near your home are ravaged so that a new highway may be built; you or a loved one are diagnosed with cancer, or heart disease, or diabetes; an old, beautiful tree in your yard has to be cut down because the branches intrude upon the electrical wires next to your property; your best friend moves away; you or a loved one has a miscarriage; a worldwide pandemic threatens every person on earth. In a word, grief is always about a significant loss.

Tagore And Gandhi

Tagore's most famous friendship, difficult though it was at times, was founded upon a mutual desire to help the Indians become a proud, independent people. Tagore and Gandhi revered each other and treasured each other's company, despite their disagreements about fundamental issues. The public debates and widely published letters between Tagore and Gandhi received the publicity of a contemporary blockbuster movie.

Some of the issues that repeatedly bubbled up during the twenty-six- year friendship between Tagore and Gandhi mirror major concerns often addressed by Tagore. The British-sponsored educational system treated the students as automatons and allowed for little independent thought and creative expression. Tagore detested this, and, in response, he founded Shantiniketan and Visva-Bharati, his primary school and university. Gandhi likewise took great exception to the existing educational opportunities, but he encouraged complete withdrawal from the state- sponsored schools.[9] Gandhi ennobled Tagore's educational experiments, but the reality was that Tagore's small, isolated schools only impacted a few students in a country of millions.

Gandhi instigated a gigantic groundswell of revolution against anything British, or inherent to western civilization. Tagore viewed this isolationist attitude as a mistake that would further drag India's multitudes into irreversible poverty, illiteracy, and complete lack of science and technology. Additionally, Tagore feared that if Indians embraced national bigotry, they would simultaneously reject the rest of the world's peoples. Tagore's life and vision were anchored in his faith in God and his belief that one's spirituality is empty without a compassionate response to the world.

[9] Bhattacharaya, Ed., 1999, pp. 7–8

God's Fault?

Our work was over for the day, and now the light was fading; We did not think that anyone would come before the morning.
All the houses round about
Dark and shuttered for the night –
One or two amongst us said, "The King of Night is coming."
We just laughed at them and said, "No one will come till morning." And when on outer doors we seemed to hear a knocking noise,
We told ourselves, "That's only the wind, they rattle when it blows."
Lamps snuffed out throughout the house, Time for rest and peacefulness –
One or two amongst us said, "His heralds are at the doors."
We just laughed and said, "The wind rattles them when it blows." And when at dead of night we heard a strange approaching clangour, We thought, sleep-fuddled as we were, it was only distant thunder.
Earth beneath us live and trembling, Stirring as if it too were waking –
One or two were saying, "Hear how the wheels of his chariot clatter." Sleepily we said, "No no, that's only distant thunder."

> And when with night still dark there rose a drumming loud and near, Somebody called to all, "Wake up, wake up, delay no more!"
> Everyone shaking now with fright, Arms wrapped close across each heart –
> Somebody cried in our ears, "O see his royal standard rear!" At last we started up and said, "We must delay no more."
> O where are the lights, the garlands, where are the signs of celebration? Where is the throne? The King has come, we made no preparation!
> Alas what shame, what destiny, No court, no robes, no finery –
> Somebody cried in our ears, "O vain, o vain this lamentation: With empty hands, in barren rooms, offer your celebration." Fling wide the doors and let him in to the lowly conch's boom; In deepest dark the King of Night has come with wind and storm.
> Thunder crashing across the skies, Lightning setting the clouds ablaze –
> Drag your tattered blankets, let the yard be spread with them:
> The King of Grief and Night has come to our land with wind and storm.
> —Tagore[10]

Tagore's poem about the unexpected arrival of the King of Night reminds me of the Christian story of Jesus's arrival into Jerusalem. In the Christian tradition, the day that we call Palm Sunday heralds an atmosphere of celebration. "Jesus is coming, Jesus is coming!" Palm Sunday represents the welcoming of Jesus a few days prior to his arrest, mock trial, beating, and crucifixion. Like the folks in Tagore's poem, we don't recognize the foreshadowing of disaster.

In 1906 when Tagore wrote this poem, that portion of India, which had been home to the Tagore family for generations, was fractionalized due to government intervention. The partition of Bengal masked a concern by the British authorities about maintaining control over the Hindu and Muslim population.[11] Public outcry against the partition had instigated a huge, potentially violent revolution.

This poem is a masterpiece about widespread denial. Like so many of the citizens of Tagore's homeland, many of us have shuttered our heart's doors to the widespread grief, which covers much of the world like a giant shadow. Whether it's about racism, religious bigotry, tribalism/nationalism, the environment, poverty, or preventable suffering, much of today's western mentality chooses to ignore the plight of the stranger, or even the neighbor down the street.

Tagore implies that the "king of grief and night" is God. In Tagore's day, as in contemporary America, I am certain that many people find that offensive. How can one claim that God is the creator of all and simultaneously deny God's involvement in destruction and sorrow? That is the central dilemma to the Christian faith. Did God require the suffering and horrendous death of his faithful and flawless servant, Jesus? Whether one is Christian, Jewish, Muslim, or Hindu, the question of God's involvement with evil remains fundamental. Despite, or perhaps because of, Tagore's lifelong confidence in God's presence, Tagore posed the issue of this conflict over and over again.

The "tattered blankets," which spread across the yard, instead of a red carpet, to welcome royalty, represent a haunting reminder that Tagore fully understood how unfair life is, especially to those who want for the most basic necessities of life. This reminds me of whatever might have happened on that Palm Sunday long ago as Jesus made his way to Jerusalem, the site of his crucifixion. If there is any historicity in the gospel description of Palm Sunday, I am certain that tattered blankets spread across the yard describes the reality of impoverished and war- weary peasants offering their best to one who they prayed would save them. The image is as true for first century Palestine, as it is for India, Rwanda, Syria, the Appalachians, or countless other places across our globe.

God often gets blamed, harassed, denied, and despised for the circumstances that lead to grief. It is human nature to blame someone when life goes awry. Blaming or questioning God are less damaging responses to grief than seeking revenge against another person or group. "The King of Grief and Night has come to our land with wind and storm." Abruptly, Tagore ends the poem with fury and destruction. Where is the healing or the hope in that? I think the fact that one can ask the hard questions, honestly and without fear of retribution, is indeed hopeful.

One of the things that concerns me the most about any religion is when the practitioner turns off one's brain in the name of worship. When faced with grievous challenges, Tagore did not shrink from challenging or questioning God. Countless seekers of the truth have suffered denigration and damnation when they have questioned the ways of God.

In my tradition, Christianity, an author far removed from Tagore also seemed to question the ways of God. Christian scriptures were canonized centuries before the discoveries in the mid-twentieth century of the Dead Sea Scrolls. Because of that, many conservative Christian organizations continue to deny biblical scholarship since 1611, when The King James Version of the Bible was published.

The most current scholarship recognizes that the oldest manuscripts for the gospel of Mark did not include any resurrection appearances of Jesus.[12] The original ending of the gospel of Mark describes three distraught women going to Jesus's tomb very early on the morning after the Sabbath. Their purpose was to wash and anoint the broken and battered body of the crucified Jesus. When they arrived at the tomb, they were frightened by an angel, who told them, "Do not be alarmed: you are looking for Jesus of Nazareth, who was crucified. He has been raised; he is not here."[13] The angel then instructed them to tell the other disciples of Jesus's resurrection. They did no such thing. "They went out and fled from the tomb, for terror and amazement had seized them; and they said nothing to anyone, for they were afraid."[14] The end.

According to the unedited manuscripts, the oldest extant gospel about Jesus stops dead right there. The terrified women told no one, and Jesus made no post-resurrection appearances. Surely, it must have seemed to those women, and to all those who had placed their greatest hopes in Jesus of Nazareth, that, in Tagore's words, "the King of Grief and Night has come to our land with wind and storm." Like Tagore, and the first followers of Jesus—all who seek wholeness for their broken hearts, regardless of the precipitating circumstance—must embrace the reality of grief and fear. One cannot bypass the storm of grief, though God knows we try.

[10] Tagore, 2005b, pp 71–2
[11] Dutta & Robinson, 2009, p.143
[12] Boring & Craddock, 2004, "Mark 16:1-8," pp. 171–172
[13] Mark 16:6, Revised Standard Version of Bible
[14] Mark 16:8, Revised Standard Version of Bible

Too Reserved For The World

> While trudging a lonely path my lamp has blown out Storm has descended – hark – storm has descended And in storm have I found my companion
> ... The path that I headed for is now lost, Where in the deep darkness do I go now?
> Perhaps this sound of thunder will speak of a new path Leading to another land ere morning turns to night
>
> —Tagore[15]

For several months during 1914 Tagore suffered significant depression, partly related to the new and unexpected pressures thrust upon him after he won the Nobel Prize for Literature. The world's doors literally opened for the poet who was hardly known outside of India. Suddenly, Tagore became a highly sought treasure. The newly famous introvert complained,

I am still suffering from Nobel Prize notoriety and I do not know what nursing home there is where I can go and get rid of this my latest and greatest trouble. To deprive me of my seclusion is like shelling an oyster – the rude touch of the curious world is all over me – I am pining for the shade of obscurity.[16]

In the Meyers-Briggs categories of personality preferences, I always tilt so much towards introversion that I fall off the scale. Introversion is the preference for solitude or near-solitude to access energy and creativity.[17] Growing up, I blended into the wall so completely that I marvel at how rich my life became. The preference for introversion, or "obscurity," as Tagore called it, seems a particularly difficult burden in 21st century America. People who choose silence and solitude instead of boardrooms and parties frequently experience a grief seldom named. Society accuses us of snobbery and not being smart enough. Sometimes, we even get stuck with psychological labels.[18] Occasionally, the stress overwhelms us so much that, like Tagore, we become physically and emotionally ill.

Prior to my career in the army, I suffered a painful year as a chaplain intern in a large metropolitan hospital. Day after day, I forced myself to walk onto hospital wards full of people I didn't know. After introducing myself as the chaplain, I prayed that the person in the bed would converse with me for a few minutes. The program paid me a pauper's pittance in return for which I was required to summarize all of my patient visits and offer written verbatim records of several of those encounters every week. I would have preferred to crawl under the bed and hide, but forcing myself to pretend that I was extraverted helped me acquire comfort with some needed people skills.

"While trudging a lonely path my lamp has blown out," wrote the poet. "The path that I headed for is now lost/Where in the deep darkness do I go now?" Tagore's dreams of living a Walden Pond type of isolation, occasionally interspersed with bouts of travel, dissolved. Tagore's preferred path of introversion collided with a new reality when he received the Nobel Prize. It led to another land, as he predicted. His travels and his acclaim inspired much of his poetry and music, and the prize money helped sustain his beloved school, at least for a short time.

Those of us who prefer "obscurity" frequently find challenges in social settings and professional settings. We generally don't like big crowds of people or noisy parties, and we are uncomfortable with meet and greet events. During my army career, I was cordially required to attend countless events that exceeded my comfort level. Many dozens of those events mandated formal wear for civilians and formal uniforms for the military members. My dressiest uniform is a full-length skirt, ruffled blouse, short bolero-style jacket, and, of course, all the ribbons and medals I earned. I looked great, but I felt uneasy about all those people I needed to greet, some of whom I was supposed to know but forgot who they were or what their job was.

And to make it much more stressful, I was almost always the sole or one of only a handful of women officers. I stood out in a crowd, like it or not. As if that weren't enough stress for this introvert, in my entire career, I can count on one hand the times I was not the only woman chaplain present. The protocol for most of those events included an invocation. There I stood, front and center, all eyes and ears waiting for Linda to look and sound professional and confident.

I cannot imagine how difficult Nobel Prize notoriety was for Tagore. Not only did he become the focus of attention everywhere he went, in his world travels, he became the ambassador for all of India. Ultimately, he rose admirably to the occasion.

Those of us who are "quiet" in a world of noise often force ourselves to learn new socialization skills.[19] I remain grateful for the opportunities that shoved me towards this new land of extraversion. My life is so much better because I no longer avoid people and events that enrich me and grow me. For many years now, I've enjoyed my "pretend extraversion"[20] when I sing for audiences, when I lead worship services, and when I teach classes and workshops. Introverts can learn extraversion skills and offer their own abilities and gifts to others in work and relaxation settings.

Persons who grieve because their socialization skills do not seem to fit the accepted norm might take comfort from the last lines of Tagore's poem. "A new path leading to another land" could point to an invention, a treasured relationship, a fresh perspective on a pesky problem or an increase in emotional contentment. Seldom does life follow the script we write; though if we stretch our comfort levels and open our hearts and minds in wonder and gratitude, we often discover a chapter we never even imagined.

[15] Tagore, 2009, p. 264
[16] Dutta & Robinson, Eds., 2005, p.137
[17] Martin, 2007, p.3
[18] Cain, 2012, p.31
[19] Cain, 2012
[20] Cain, 2012

Song And Dance

Maybe, I got lost somewhere along the way. I remember feeling so confident about God's presence for much of my childhood and youth. Now, when I forget, God's messengers occasionally peek through the curtains of my memory like a tiny sliver of light.

I can hear two little girls laughing and singing while they splash around in a wading pool on a hot Oklahoma summer's evening in the mid-1950s. My younger sister and I grew up singing together, frequently improvising melodies and harmonies, letting the songs waft and curl like incense floating to heaven. That night, at least as I recall it from over half a century, Sharon and I baptized our backyard with water and music. Immersed in the moment, unaware of looming Cold War with Russia, or the concerns of a young preacher and his wife for their family, Sharon and I hopped up and down and warbled like two enchanted nightingales. I looked up into the starry sky, and there they were: angels dancing, celebrating life with two carefree children.

For years, I have wanted to participate once again in the angels' joy. That memory, which may have been a dream rather than "reality," is one of the times in my life when I felt joined to the universe. I knew without doubt that I belonged to All That Is. Those precious experiences re- membered me with everyone and every creature, and every mountain and river and star, throughout all time and space.

Tagore's writings describe many divine ecstasies during his life, almost always associated with an experience in nature.

> One day I was out in a boat on the Ganges. It was a beautiful evening in autumn. The sun had just set; the silence of the sky was full to the brim with ineffable peace and beauty.... Suddenly a big fish leapt up to the surface of

the water and then disappeared, displaying on its vanishing figure all the colours of the evening sky. . . . It came up from the depths of its mysterious dwelling with a beautiful dancing motion and added its own music to the silent symphony of the dying day. I felt as if I had a friendly greeting from an alien world in its own language, and it touched my heart with a flash of gladness.[21]

Hundreds of Tagore's poems and song lyrics center on his faith in God and his recognition of holiness everywhere. The painful thing about having that kind of mystical experience, like the angels I saw singing and dancing, is that we want to live there. The human experience scatters all manner of challenges and hurts along the way. We can choose to learn from them or not. "Sin," concluded Tagore, "is an attitude . . . that our self is the ultimate truth, and that we are not all essentially one but exist each for his own separate individual existence."[22] Tagore's definition of sin crystalizes what I consider one of the most dangerous attitudes of humankind: that my own expectation or experience of holiness is the standard to which others should aspire. Whether we feel touched with gladness, as Tagore described the beautiful dancing fish, or whether an angel dances with us, whatever experience that reminds us of the numinous and the ineffable mystery merits only one response: heartfelt gratitude.

Throughout his life, Rabindranath's daily practice included early morning meditations and prayers based on the ancient Vedas and devotional songs of his own creation. From childhood, Tagore learned the famous and beloved Vedic prayer called the Gayatri. He nurtured this verse as his daily mantra throughout his life.[23] Tagore nestled these powerful words into music, thus even further deepening this prayer into his heart and soul. One of the most familiar translations of this prayer for self-realization is the following: "Let us meditate on the brilliant light of that one who is worthy of worship and who has created all worlds! May he direct our minds to the truth."[24]

I have received great strength and comfort from prayers and devotional songs, from Hindu and Christian traditions as well as Native American, Jewish, and Muslim heritages. Sometimes, the prayers and songs were not formally composed and will likely never be repeated, but the angels always hear them. And dancing happens.

"Wolf Sister"

by Linda George

Like an ancient sound from deep within the earth, Like a breath sighing the universe,
Like a shadow in the moonlight, I've always known you, my Sister. Your fears of annihilation, of torture, Cause my heart to quiver.
I weep with you
When your mate and children and tribe suffer.
We are so much alike – humans and wolves.
Despite our masks of strength and will,
When we listen to the starlight, We touch our vulnerabilities, Our need for one another,
Our prayers for compassion instead of competition. The banquet table of my soul
Will always reserve a seat for you, my Friend.
I long to meet you beneath the shadows of the moon, So that we may share our songs
And dream our dances.

[21] Dutta & Robinson, 2009, p. 174-5
[22] Dutta & Robinson, 2009, p. 175
[23] Tagore, 2005b, pp. 172–3
[24] Friedrichs, 1986, "Gayatri," p. 117

Hope In The Darkness

Hold thy faith firm, my heart, the day will dawn,
The seed of promise is deep in the soil, it will sprout.
Sleep, like a bud, will open its heart to the light, and the silence will find its voice.
The day is near when thy burden will become thy gift, and thy sufferings will light up thy path.

—Tagore[25]

The images in the preceding poem describe darkness birthing new life: a faithful heart dawning with new light; a buried seed sprouting through the dark soil; sleep enshrouded in a bud, like a flower opening to the sun; and those whose voices have been deadened finding their way to a new form of expression. Tagore promises that the heavy burdens will become gifts, and the sources of suffering will light the darkened path.

By the time Tagore wrote this poem, death had scarred his heart many times. One wonders if Tagore composed this poem as a mantra of hope for himself. One can feel Tagore's encouragement and trust that life's difficulties will resolve, even though the how and the why are unknown.

"The day is near when thy burden will become thy gift, and thy sufferings will light up thy path."

Those who have survived to the other side of grief, and those who remain blissfully ignorant of the pain of grief need to exert great care in trying to comfort another. How many times I remember well-intentioned people who care about me suggesting that everything will be okay. Perhaps it will, and perhaps it won't. The only person who can assert that the burden has become a gift is the one who suffers. In my case, and in Tagore's case, the burden has indeed transformed into a gift that lights the path. Whether that happens, how that happens and how long it takes to happen, are subjective to each person and each specific grief-inducing event.

How did Tagore find the strength to continue in the shadow of so much sorrow and despair? How did he find light amidst such darkness? And what about the rest of us, whose experiences of profound grief may number considerably fewer than Tagore's? Must we also suffer such unimaginable losses to find the gift in the burden? I realize that many people in our broken world experience more suffering than seems humanly possible. In my opinion, Tagore was one of those. What I would never suggest is that we are somehow emotionally or spiritually deficient without numerous tragedies in our lives.

Tagore believed that experiencing sorrow enables one to "confront oneself."[26] I certainly agree with that statement, though I would never offer it as balm to someone following a significant loss. A year after his wife died, Tagore wrote some poems commemorating her. In one of them, he cries out to God about the emptiness in his life.

> No, no, she's no longer in my house!
> I've looked in every corner. Nowhere to be found .
> . . But [Y]our house is infinite, all-pervasive,
> And it's there, Lord, I've come to look for her.
> Here I stand, beneath this evening sky,
> And look at [Y]ou, tears streaming from my eyes.
> There's a place from where no face, no bliss,
> No hope, no thirst can ever be snatched from us.
> It's there I've brought my devastated heart. . .
> —Tagore[27]

Reading these anguished, pleading words, one cannot suggest that Tagore hid from suffering. People sometimes believe that Kubler-Ross's "stages of grief"[28] are literal, separate, and measurable, like walking up a flight of stairs. There, I've completed that step, and now I'm moving to the next one. That kind of thinking represents a total misunderstanding of Kubler-Ross's research. She understood, perhaps better than most of us, that grief does not happen like that.

Grieving more closely resembles being stuck in a gigantic blender, in which all the emotions you've ever felt, and some that you've never felt, get mixed together. You can be assured that different emotions are going to pop to the top during the process. Anger may take priority for an instant, or a day, and then sadness, or resentment, or fear, or even humor, may take over. The thing that's so frightening and disconcerting is that there's no predicting how you will feel at any given time, what the catalyst might be, or when it will happen.

Here are the key factors that I think enabled Tagore to live in the ambiguity of grief and find a way through it. From his early teens and every day for the rest of his life, except when he was comatose and near death, he spent time in meditation and prayer every morning and every evening. Although he consistently asked the hard questions of "why" in his poems and prayers, he did not pretend to know the answers.[29] What he did know was a personal relationship with God, whom he called his Jeevan Devata (Supreme Being). That One "…helped me come to terms with my life's joys and sorrows and to unite me with the universe."[30]

Although Tagore often had challenges relating intimately with people in a face-to- face encounter, he revealed much vulnerability and candor about himself in his letters and his poems. In her book, *Daring Greatly*, Brene Brown explores how frequently society seems to emphasize the mindset that allowing vulnerability equals being a "loser," and a victim. Staying in control, dominating, and exerting power apparently epitomize the qualities of success.[31]

When Rabindranath prayed and sang and wrote, he trusted God to treasure and guide him so that the poet could share his emotions, even the uncomfortable ones. Tagore's discipline of mindful prayer and meditation enabled him to open his heart, not only to God, but to millions of grateful readers. The relationships that Tagore nurtured, with those seen and unseen, gave him the courage to expose his grief and fragility. I do not believe that anyone who consistently hides his or her grief from self and others can experience any healing.

Brokenness doesn't disappear just because it's hidden behind a strong or beautiful facade.

I believe that those who feel loved and welcomed and who believe in their own worthiness are also those who can honor their grief. Tagore always believed that God cherished him and everyone else; thus, Tagore could weep for his departed loved ones while he proclaimed a message of hope. "The day is near when your burden will become your gift, and your sufferings will light up your path."

[25] Tagore, 2011a, #12 in "Crossing, p. 222
[26] Som, 2009, p. 82
[27] Tagore, 1995, #5, in "Smaran," p. 127
[28] Kubler-Ross, 2007, "Stages of Grief"
[29] Kripalani, 2008, p. 484
[30] Tagore, 2006, p. 322
[31] Brown, 2012, pp. 151–2

Patriotism That Isolates

In 1903, the British viceroy Lord Curzon considered the proposal of a full-scale partition of Bengal, which included much of northern India at the time. Tagore and generations of his family had called Bengal home. The undivided province totaled 189,000 square miles, with a population exceeding 78 million.[32] Massive fears and frustrations among British and Indian landowners and politicians surrounded this action. What the privileged few had not considered was the sense of unity among the Bengali-speaking people. Racial discrimination, arrogance, and public humiliations against the Indians were prevalent. The Bengali revolution became known as the Swadeshi (home rule) movement and lasted for five years.[33]

> My golden Bengal, it's you I adore.
> Your sky, your air, play flute forever in my soul. . .
> Oh Ma, your herder, your farmers, they're all
>   brothers of my soul. Oh Ma, at your feet
>   my head I've laid --
> Give me your foot-dust, it'll be jewel on my head.
> Oh Ma, whatever poor man's treasure I [have] I
>   will place at your feet --
> Oh, I could die for it.
>
> —Tagore[34]

Tagore's grief during this time in his life embraced those closest to him, as well as the national anguish of his motherland. Many of the better-educated Hindus of Bengal, including Tagore, felt betrayed and angry. Initially, Tagore took a leadership role in the protests that would herald Gandhi's famous Noncooperation Movement two decades later. By 1907, the violence between Bengali Hindus and Muslims, and bomb attacks against British officials, disturbed Tagore so much that he withdrew from the movement.[35] He endured tremendous criticism for advocating human dignity and respect over and above provincial patriotism.

Tagore worked for years in the fields of education and rural reconstruction, trying to assimilate the best of the West and India. In a radical departure from the norm of early 20th century India, Tagore sent his son and son-in-law to the University of Illinois for training in agriculture. They returned to teach rural Bengali farmers how to improve their crops.[36]

Tagore never stopped loving his homeland ("Ma" in his poem), but he refused to claim that India could be, or should be, self-reliant. This topic became a huge source of disagreement between him and his friend Gandhi. Many years later, Tagore's son asserted, "It was impossible for [Father] to accept what he called 'the passion for rejection' as an ideal."[37]

Amid his profound grief over the ripping apart of his beloved Bengal, Tagore reached out to the powerful politicians and begged them to recognize the moral and spiritual greatness of Bengal. Unlike Gandhi, India's most famous proponent of home rule, Tagore refused to vilify all things British. Whether they were impoverished, illiterate villagers or privileged products of British education, whether they were Hindu, Sikh, Christian, or Muslim, Tagore asserted that Bengalis regarded each other as family. "It is my conviction that my countrymen will gain truly their India by fighting against that education which teaches them that a country is greater than the ideals of humanity."[38]

I also grieve the direction my homeland is heading. So many young people in our armed forces are suffering and dying, ostensibly for freedom and democracy. I fear they are suffering for causes less noble, such as maintaining economic and military status. Having served in our military for twenty-four years, I feel great pride and hope in our military members. Although my politics and theology often differ from many of those in uniform, I know that these folks lay down their lives for the rest of us— not because they seek hero status, but because they believe in the principles, which form the foundation of democracy: respect and nurture for all persons.

I do love my country, warts and all, even as Tagore loved his homeland. I also share with Tagore a profound sense of concern and grief that nationalistic pride must not blind us to the truths and gifts and sufferings of the entire world. The patriotic poems and songs that Tagore wrote represent a minuscule portion of his entire corpus. After a few years of being in the forefront of Indian fervor, Tagore declined to participate in that energy, because he recognized how much dissension and bigotry it was causing. Many people faulted him for his unwillingness to promote India at all costs.

"Rabindranath felt increasingly dissatisfied with the character that the political agitation was assuming -- its narrow political aims, disregard for the wider perspective of social and economic regeneration and Hindu chauvinism placing motherland as God."[39]

On my car is a bumper sticker which has inspired complete strangers to stop me and ask where I got it. The words "God bless all nations" sit atop a dozen or so symbols of the world's spiritual traditions. This bumper sticker represents my heart's prayer. I'm certain Tagore was confident of God's compassion for all nations. Perhaps, the better prayer is: "May the people of all nations bless one another."

[32] Sarkar, 2010, pp. 8–11
[33] Sarkar, 2010
[34] Tagore, 2008b, pp. 307–309
[35] Dutta & Robinson, Eds., 2005, pp. 61–2
[36] Das Gupta, 2013, pp. 93–9
[37] Dutta & Robinson, Eds., 2005, p. 62
[38] Tagore, 2006, pp. 156–7
[39] Som, 2009, p. 102

Grief is Messy

Sadness, anger, fear, anxiety, guilt – all of those emotions are uncomfortable—too often described as "negative." When any one of them, or a cluster of them, becomes a person's predominant response to life, a tenuous and even dangerous situation threatens. Likewise, a life devoid of those difficult emotions, or one that denies those emotions, may be equally fragile. All those emotions are part of being human, and all of them contribute to this amorphous experience called grief. Grief is messy, complicated, unpredictable, and often lonely.[40]

When we erect a wall of safety around our messy emotions, when the only emotions we allow reflect happiness or anger, we dig ourselves into a deep well of isolation. We isolate ourselves from our own truth, our own souls, and we may isolate ourselves from those around us.[41]

Tagore would unhesitatingly acknowledge that many body/soul blows throughout his life temporarily incapacitated him, and several times threatened to crush him. Never would he romanticize or minimize the difficulty of a tornado barreling through his life.

For several months in 1926 and 1927, Tagore traveled in Europe and Asia, meeting people, learning about their daily lives, and interacting with their leaders. His hopes for world peace and reconciliation collided with reality. Shortly after Tagore's return home, a Muslim fanatic assassinated a Hindu reformer in Delhi. Tagore told the instructors in his school, "The greatest calamity which afflicts us in this country is that different communities should be dwelling side by side and yet have no real relations with one another."[42]

Much of the publicity surrounding Tagore's appearances and lectures in other parts of Europe and China antagonized non-Asians and practically halted the donations he so desperately needed to support his school, which by this time included a university.[43] With so many difficult assaults aimed at Tagore in such a narrow window of time, I think anyone could understand his reactions and anguish.

After my former husband Jerry died in an automobile accident, so many people tried to offer explanations of why this tragedy had happened. I barely had the energy to feel angry, and, fortunately, I did not believe their explanations: God was trying to make me stronger; Jerry was much happier now; I was going to be happier and fulfilled in the future; "Satan" was having his way; God was using this to warn nonbelievers they'd better get saved. I wanted to tell them to shut up. I wanted someone to care about me enough to sit with me and hold my hand. I wanted someone to let me cry when I needed to, which was most of the time, and sometimes let me laugh without making me feel guilty. My grief was deeper than words. My emotions were as raw and exposed and fragile as third-degree burns.

The greatest gift to me during that time happened when someone allowed my tears without trying to console me. When no words could make things better, and someone sat with me in silence, I did not feel so alone, and holiness enshrouded us.

Tagore's writings are filled with questions and anguish, which may not seem like hope.

> Today, who has filled my flute's empty heart with pain, With tune that shatters easy comforts, a tune of detaching.
> The eager flute itself makes the home-leaver restless –
> Calls from the near to the far, calls in dream, calls in waking,
> The one that hiding in my soul's remote corner makes me cry in the dusk hour –
> the name still unknown to me, the visage still of no familiarity – yet the shadowy presence constantly wanders in my dream.
> —Tagore[44]

When grief moves into one's heart and seems to consume every waking and sleeping moment, perhaps the only consolation is to embrace the grief. It's not the same consolation as chocolate, or alcohol, or mindless television or video games. Intentionally journeying through the sadness, the hurt, the despair, the loneliness, and the fear allows one to catch a glimpse of daylight, like the tiniest sliver peeking through a heavy curtain. Perhaps, one day, the curtain will open more fully. Hiding or minimizing or denying the intense pain guarantees that one will remain stranded in a fog, addicted to pretense and lies. There is no way to get around the truth that grief is messy. It "shatters easy comforts . . . makes me cry . . . [and] constantly wanders in my dream."

40 Greenspan, 2004
41 Greenspan, 2004
42 Dutta & Robinson, p. 274
43 Kripalani, 2008, pp. 358–62
44 Tagore, 2008b, pp. 242–3

Don't Give Up

My husband Wayne has cancer. He has had distressing symptoms for almost two years, and numerous doctors and tests failed to discover why. Now, we know that his cancer is aggressive and has been growing for some time. My feelings, fears, and frustrations are gnawing away at me as surely as a disease. I cannot continue this negative downward spiral, or I will get sick and be unable to help my husband through the awful treatments and surgery he faces. This grief in which I am currently dog-paddling is different from the other grief-inducing experiences in my life. I, of course, know that every experience of grief has its own volition and personality. Grieving is sometimes like getting sucked into a storm-wracked kaleidoscope. The prism of emotions swirl dizzyingly like multiple colors and shapes, and the infinite ways in which they interact are as unpredictable as a sudden bout of stomach flu.

After his beloved wife died, C.S. Lewis observed that he never knew that grief felt so much like fear.[45] I have felt tremendous fear surrounding Wayne's diagnosis. The location and type of his cancer could easily spread to his lymph nodes and other vital organs. His treatment plan requires an especially aggressive and violent counter-attack. That alone is enough to frighten me into a cesspool of doubt. What I think is gurgling underneath the obvious fear are the memories of losing my former husband. Even though I have felt at peace for many years about Jerry's death, the memories of the anguish and fear can still cause my heart to lurch. My grief throughout that period encompassed so many losses.

Six weeks after I buried Jerry, I drove halfway across the country to a huge metropolitan area where I knew no one. I moved into a house that Jerry and I had purchased a few months earlier, in preparation for our upcoming military assignments to the Washington, DC, area. It was years before ordinary folks could purchase a Global Positioning System, and between my exhausted and muddled state of mind and my terminal geographic impairment, I never would have found the house except for the kindness of the realtor. The house seemed to overflow with unpacked boxes full of ghosts and a seemingly unending assortment of items that needed to be reassembled—little things like tables and chairs and bookcases and the washing machine. On a good day, I can hit the head of a nail with a hammer. And if I don't have to go any higher than the second step of a stepstool, I can change a light bulb. That's pretty much the extent of my handyman abilities.

A couple of days after I arrived at my new home, I started my job in the world's largest office building, the Pentagon. During my first day of in- processing, a young clerk filling out the mandatory forms asked for my marital status. I told her that my husband had died in a car accident six weeks earlier. I guess I looked professional in my uniform, and I was not weeping then, so she asked me "Are you over it already?" A few days later, a senior staff officer who knew of Jerry's death asked me, "Has this changed your life?"

When my random bouts of crying prompted me to explain my situation to yet another stranger, she told me, "You're lucky. At least your husband wasn't cheating on you." Another time, a man I encountered in the hallways told me I should smile, because he had never seen a chaplain who seemed so gloomy. He thought he knew me because he could see the chaplain insignia on my collar. He could not see my broken heart.

Besides losing my husband, my home, and my friends, I did not know how to get to and from the grocery store or the doctor's office or all the other daily life errands. The only reason I could make it to and from work every day, is because I caught a bus, almost right outside my front door. Every time I got in my car, I feared that I would not be able to find my way back home.

I felt lost without our two large, beloved dogs. The heat prevented me from transporting them for several months. I also seemed to lose my mind. I could not remember anything! Many times, I literally stopped in the middle of a sentence, drawing a complete blank about what I was saying. Hundreds of times I went into a room with a purpose, only to stop stock still without a clue why I was there. Years later, one of the women with whom I had worked at the Pentagon reported that she told her supervisor, "There's something wrong with that new chaplain." Yes, there certainly was.

The pain, the loneliness, the fear—the massive ocean of uncertainty in which I was drowning—all seemed bent on destroying me. A few months later, a routine mammography suggested another sinister plot. One of my new friends generously offered to accompany me to the requisite follow-up ultrasound.

One after another, a parade of medical people came into the examining room. Each of them moved the instrument over my bare breast while studying the monitor in the semi-darkened room. Nobody spoke to the increasingly frightened woman barely clad in a sheet. Then a doctor came in and pronounced that the culprit was merely a cyst. "Get another mammogram in six months," he said as he rushed out to see another patient. An angel dressed as a nurse came in shortly to find me sobbing. She hugged me and escorted me back to the waiting room. I saw the terror in my friend's eyes when I returned to the waiting room, red-eyed and aided by a nurse. Then we all shared tears of joy.

When Jerry died so unexpectedly, immediately followed by my moving halfway across the country, I became a stranger in a strange land. The primary advice to a person grieving a significant loss is to talk to friends about one's feelings, thoughts, memories, and concerns. In my new neighborhood, my new church, and my new job, I literally had no friends who knew Jerry, and they had only met me. Long-distance phone calls, and cards and letters helped to sustain me day to day, but they were a poor substitute for sitting with a loved one, sharing tears, laughter, and hugs. I remain eternally grateful for the many strangers whose courage enabled them to step into their own fears and approach this frightened, weary woman they did not know and offer her love and safety.

Wayne's cancer diagnosis stirs up memories and fears, but this grief is completely different from when Jerry died. Wayne and I have lived in the same city and the same home for seven years now—the longest time I've lived anywhere in one place for thirty years. We have many friends here, and their outreach to us since Wayne's diagnosis continues to amaze, strengthen, and gratify us.

The aggressive treatment plan for Wayne includes almost daily radiation and chemotherapy simultaneously for several weeks, followed by a six- or seven-hour surgery to remove part of his stomach and most of his esophagus. The medical team are keeping us informed of what we need to know for the immediate present, without overwhelming us with details about the long-term recovery. Both of us are trying to keep our focus on the present, acknowledging the giftedness of each day.

Whether one is facing a health crisis, or bankruptcy, or a crushed relationship, or countless other grief-inducing situations, it is so easy to allow our fears of the unknown to pummel our minds, bodies, and spirits.

Tagore experienced that in his life many times as he struggled to make sense of the insensible, and as he struggled to find peace in his soul. In one of his poems, he offers encouragement to a lone bird struggling against all odds to fly across the nighttime ocean.

> Though the evening's coming with slow and languid steps, All music's come to a halt, as if at a cue,
> In the endless sky there's none else to fly with you,
> And weariness is descending on your breast, though a great sense of dread throbs unspoken,
> And all around you the horizon is draped, yet bird, o my bird, Already blind, don't fold your wings yet...
> Ahead of you still stretches a long, long night; The sun has gone to sleep behind a mountain. The universe – it seems to hold its

> breath, Sitting quietly, counting the passing hours.
> And now on the dim horizon a thin curved moon,
> Swimming against obscurity, appears.
> Bird, o my bird, already blind, don't fold your wings yet. Above you the stars have spread their fingers,
> As in a mime, with a meaning in their gaze.
> Below you death – deep, leaping, restless – Snarls at you in a hundred thousand waves. But on a far shore some are pleading with you, 'Come, come': their wailing prayer says.
> So bird, o my bird, already blind, don't fold your wings yet. . .
>
> —Tagore[46]

Don't give up, regardless of the seeming impossibilities that assault you. "On a far shore some are pleading with you, 'Come, come.'" The message applies to everyone who feels as though she or he is drowning in grief, depression, anxiety, or fear. Keep going, don't give up. Someone— perhaps, unknown to you—is pleading for your survival.

For a long time after Jerry's death, I could not sing. Like Tagore, I have sung my entire life, and the music cleanses my soul, and heals me, and fills me with joy, contemplation, peace. After Jerry died, instead of melody, only sobs escaped my lips. Now, I find it difficult once again to sing. Partly that's because singing is such a whole-body, physical activity that requires plenty of breath, good posture, and mindfulness. The bigger reason I can't sing is because it exposes my soul, and I can't bear that right now.

Since Wayne's diagnosis, my mind and body feel constantly deprived of deep rest and deep breaths. Keeping my thoughts focused on whatever task is at hand is often as difficult as describing the color of the sky to someone who has been blind from birth. Like the little bird in Tagore's poem—blinded by the darkness and silenced in fear—I lurch through the dark storm of Wayne's cancer, unknowns leaping towards me like wild ocean waves. Tagore's poem comforts me and reminds me that I am not alone.

On a far shore some are pleading with you, 'Come, come': their wailing prayer says.

So bird, o my bird, already blind, don't fold your wings yet.

[45] Lewis, 1976, p. 1
[46] Tagore, 1995, pp. 118–9

Proving My Worth

One of the looming psychological hindrances that afflicts many of us is the fear of not doing enough and/or not being enough. The day after I began my retirement from the army, I suffered a lonely pity party, fearing that my twenty-four-year career had meant nothing—that it didn't matter, that I didn't matter. I was not sad about no longer donning the uniform and boots every day. I just felt inadequate, wondering if my life and ministry in the army truly served people and God.

So many touch points in life send us into a dark place of self-doubt and incrimination. Could I, should I have done more, acted better, paid closer attention, said more, said less? And the more we think about it, the more suffocating it becomes: an endless, not so merry-go-round of moping and misgivings.

> Guardian of Life, you nurture us
> In little cages of fragmented time,
> Boundaries to all our games, limits to all renown.
>   Today I stand before you without illusion:
> I do not ask at your door for immortality
> For the many days and nights I have spent weav-
>   ing you garlands.
> But if I have given true value
> To my small seat in a tiny segment of one of the
>   eras . . .
> Before I am utterly forgotten
> Let me place my homage at your feet.
>   —Tagore[47]

The poet was seventy-five years old and feeling his age. He was tired and not in good health. The future of the school for which he had dedicated his life seemed in peril. I feel so much pain for this man who questioned whether his life had any worth.

I am in good health, and I can certainly identify with Tagore's grief about whether or not his life has offered meaning to others. I feel that since I've been retired for several years. Tagore never retired, though his endeavors seldom met the accepted criteria for a traditional profession.

Like so many active retirees in this country, I struggle with defining myself now. Identifying myself as retired seems to suggest to many that my main goals in life focus upon visiting grandchildren, traveling, or just doing nothing. Traveling sounds great, but Wayne's ongoing health issues make that seem less and less likely. I watch with sadness as my dear husband grieves that we cannot travel from northern Virginia to southern Texas to visit his family, including the grandchildren.

My prayer echoes Tagore's, "Before I am utterly forgotten/ let me place my homage at your feet." We don't think of kneeling at someone's feet, as is common in many Eastern countries, but the gesture symbolizes the kneeler's humility and respect for another. Before I, Linda, become incapacitated or die, please, God, help me create an homage that will honor you and inspire others.

I feel sad because I don't want the main line of my obituary to read "retired army chaplain who also sang."

If I have given true value to my small seat in a tiny segment [of life]. . . If I have won from the trials of life a scrap of success . . . .

Before I am utterly forgotten, let me place my homage at your feet.

I want the last decades of my life to incorporate my work and learnings about Tagore, so that others will feel that they are worthy. I feel sad that a man as amazing and compassionate as Tagore felt unworthy. For his sake, and for those whose lives he might touch through my teachings, I offer myself.

"THE PRINCIPAL"
by Linda George
(Dedicated to Tagore)

Wrinkled fingers
Swollen knuckles
Yellow fingernails chipped and cracked. Veins bulging green
Little pinkie shaped like a warped pointer stick Skin as translucent as chalk dust.
His hands used to write letters to parents, And awards,
And decision-making documents. Now his hands tremble so much He can barely hold a coffee cup.
Tears rain down on the County Gazette,
Dissolving the news and his dreams. School bells toll in the distance –
Or is it a funeral knell?

[47] Tagore, 2005b, pp. 99–101

Gifts Offered, But Rejected

For as long as I can remember, I nurtured a confidence that I would grow into a quality musician, and that I would offer healing music to people who needed it. Some of my earliest memories find me in front of the piano. To prevent my feet dangling off the piano bench, my first piano teacher placed thick books on the floor. Instinctively, I knew, even as a preschooler, that music would companion me throughout my life. Not only did playing the piano challenge and excite me, the dream of creating beautiful music inspired me. The quality and depth of music I imagined does not surrender to mere wishful-thinking or a few years of lessons. The music I yearned to enliven requires life experience and soul-searching. That music—the music of the masters such as Beethoven, Tchaikovsky, and Chopin—also mandates decades of disciplined study as well as a pliant heart.

I have always believed that my musical abilities and passion for music are gifts from God. I remain extraordinarily grateful that my parents determined the musical training of their three daughters to be a priority. From my birth until I left home for college, we moved seven times spanning five states. Every time, one of the first things my mother did after unpacking the kitchen was to locate music teachers for us girls. I understand now that squeezing the extra dollars out of Daddy's salary to pay for private lessons required some other sacrifices of which I remained blissfully unaware.

Momma and Daddy both loved when I would play hymns. Daddy would often sing along, much to my irritation. "I'm trying to practice," I would tell him, "and when you sing or whistle with me, it messes me up." After a few years, though, I could play any hymn in the hymnal as easily as playing a children's tune from my first piano book.

I might be working on a piece by Mozart or Debussy, and Momma would ask me to play a hymn. "I don't want to play a hymn, that's too boring," I'd respond, with typical adolescent sensitivity. Years later, when some of life's storms rocked my foundation, I would caress the keyboard with those hymns, while tears coursed down my cheeks like liquid prayers.

Love for God and music intertwined throughout my entire life, as surely as love for God and music propelled Tagore's life. About four decades after my first piano lessons, I started studying vocal technique. I yearned to sing well.

Ever since I began singing solos for various audiences, I have repeatedly heard adults recount why they no longer sing. The stories are remarkably similar. When they were children or teenagers, they enjoyed singing until one day a trusted adult or friend, or perhaps a stranger, mocked their singing, or told them not to sing in public anymore. I taught a class called "Singing for Fun" for several years. We met once a week for ninety minutes and sang all sorts of Americana music that spans the years and musical styles, and we had lots of fun. Most of my class members were older than me. They were all active retirees. Their careers and life experiences encompassed the gamut from teachers to medical professionals to scientists to military veterans to gardeners and artists. What I found terribly sad was that many of these folks thought they couldn't and shouldn't sing. Frequently, I heard that Thursday afternoon became one of their favorite times of the week, when we joined our voices in song. "It's therapy," they told me.

One of the issues that grieved Tagore concerned the absence or minimization of the creative arts in the public schools. Central to the curriculum and daily activities at the primary school Tagore founded were music, dance, drama, and storytelling. He believed that the creative arts not only enhanced and encouraged learning, but that they were crucial for healthy emotional and spiritual development. He also took the children from his school to neighboring rural villages, whose populations suffered extreme despair, illiteracy, and poverty, and helped them revive their folk music and dance.[48]

For many years now, we've seen the gradual disappearance of the creative arts from most of the public schools in the United States. I am grieved by that. I think the increase in school violence, gang activity, and the dropout rate correlate with the absence of instruction and encouragement in healthy, positive, creative arts.

In 1894, Tagore published a poem about an aging singer who fears that a younger, more technically trained singer will be his demise. The older man had sung many times for the king, whose heart and soul were nurtured by the music. When the younger vocalist debuted in the court, most of the audience cheered his skill and virtuosity. The king, unmoved, requested a song from his old friend. The poem continues:

> [The aged singer] white-haired, white turban on his head, Bows to the assembled courtiers and slowly takes his seat. He takes the tanpura in his wasted, heavily veined hand And with lowered head and closed eyes begins [singing]. His quavering voice is swallowed by the enormous hall,
> It is like a tiny bird in a storm, unable to fly for all it tries. . . The courtiers are inattentive, some whisper amongst themselves, Some of them yawn, some doze, some go off to their rooms;
> Some of them call to servants, "Bring the hookah, bring some pan"...
> Music that should rise on its own joy from the depths of his heart Is crushed by heedless clamor . . .
> His voice quakes with distress, like a lamp guttering in a breeze. He abandons the words of the song and tries to salvage the tune, But suddenly his wide-mouthed singing breaks

Healing

> into loud cries. . . He has failed to remember a song; he weeps as he did as a child. With brimming eyes [the king] touches his friend:
>
> "Come, let us go from here," he says with kindness and love. They leave that festive hall with its hundreds of blinding lights. The two old friends go outside, holding each other's hands.
>
> [The singer] says with hands clasped, "Master, . . .
>
> Don't ask anyone to listen to me now, I beg you at your feet, my lord." The singer alone does not make a song, there has to be someone who hears:
>
> One man opens his throat to sing, the other sings in his mind.
>
> Only when waves fall on the shore do they make a harmonious sound; Only when breezes shake the woods do we hear a rustling in the leaves. Only from a marriage of two forces does music arise in the world.
>
> Where there is no love, where listeners are dumb, there never can be song.
>
> —Tagore[49]

According to many accounts, Tagore possessed an extraordinary singing ability. From the time he was a child, and throughout the remainder of his life, individuals and audiences repeatedly asked him to sing for them. With rare exception, the melodies and lyrics he offered were his own creation. Like the king in Tagore's poem, those who heard Tagore sing, were deeply moved.[50]

"The singer alone does not make a song, there has to be someone who hears." Many of the children and young people in our schools, like the heartbroken singer in Tagore's poem, vainly try to offer their gifts of creativity and are criticized or rejected. The internet/multi-technology epidemic of inappropriate and highly personal pronouncements, editorials, and abuse reflect the sadness, loneliness, fears, and anger of persons who believe that no one wants to hear them. These pervasive expressions of low self-esteem may be the most dangerous, contagious epidemic of 21st century America. Bullying, racism, gender identity discrimination, and ethnic antagonism among our children and young people are rampant and apparently contagious. "Where there is no love, where listeners are dumb, there never can be song."

Love is a word that is too easy to bandy about, and too hard to describe. Tagore shied from sharing his heart with a lot of people, especially after the Nobel Prize turned him into a celebrity. What I know without doubt, though, is that Tagore loved those children who lived and learned at his little school. Repeatedly, in his letters and conversations, one can sense his unbounded joy and gratitude for those children. When Tagore sang for them, or wrote a play for them, or told them a story, they knew he loved them. They heard him with their hearts and minds and spirits. And love flowed through that space as surely as healing streams of water in a parched land.[51]

Whenever and wherever the creative arts are offered and received in a spirit of love and gratitude, the givers and the recipients catch a wisp of healing as surely as a poignant melody, a striking drawing, or a touching poem.

[48] Pearson, 2010, pp. 1–17
[49] Tagore, 2005b, pp. 53–55
[50] Som, 2009, p. 132
[51] Pearson, 2010, p. 12

Following My Own Path

> Little firefly, with what abandon have you spread
>   your two wings! In the dusky twilight, in
>   the midst of the forest,
> You have poured out your heart in joy
> You are not the sun, nor the moon, yet this does
>   not diminish your happiness
> You have fulfilled yourself and lit your own flame
> What is yours is only yours -- you owe nothing
>   to anyone-- You have followed the
>   compulsions of your inner strength
> Arise above the constraints of darkness,
> You are small and yet not small
> You have adopted as your own, all the light of
>   this world.
>
> —Tagore[52]

How much joy, contentment, and gratitude we could gain if we adopt the philosophy of the firefly in this poem! I have lit my flame and followed the compulsions of my inner strength. I am small and yet not small. I have adopted as my own, all the light of this world.

One evening while in India, as I walked in the semidarkness, I looked up into a tree along the pathway. I thought the upper branches of the tree had transformed into stars. I stopped still to study this sight, and then I realized that one tree, unlike the other nearby trees, sheltered thousands of fireflies. On subsequent evenings, I observed the same twinkling celebration in that tree. I have no idea why the fireflies seemed drawn to that tree. Perhaps, that tree followed its own path to nurture the fireflies.

The fireflies followed their life's path, and the memory of that sparkling tree never fails to flood me with joy, like a searchlight on a dark night. Assuredly, I don't always do enough or be enough. I reach for something—a goal, an idea, an emotion—whose time is not now or whose attainment is not for me. And instead of celebrating who I am at the moment, I berate myself or compare myself with another. Then I hear Tagore whispering to me, as to the firefly, "You are not the sun, nor the moon, yet this does not diminish your happiness. . . You have adopted as your own, all the light of this world." Yes!

[52] Tagore, in Som, 2009, pp. 250–1

Prayer Time

At least from the time of Rabindranath's grandfather, the Tagore family enjoyed the prestige of their Brahmin caste, despite the fact that the family was ostracized centuries earlier. According to legend, the Tagore purity suffered a permanent stain when some orthodox Hindu Tagore ancestors shared a meal with Muslims. Society of that time deemed such an action intolerable, and punishments were severe. The branch of the family from which Rabindranath descended became known as *Pirali* Brahmins and could no longer intermarry with orthodox Hindus.[53] The *Jorasanko* Tagore's, as the "tainted" branch of the family came to be known, experienced prejudicial mistreatment. The male leaders of the family grew stronger in the face of societal and financial difficulty. I think that tension enabled Rabindranath's grandfather and father to push harder against the prevailing currents of the time.

Tagore, like his father and grandfather, followed a path of Hinduism called Brahmo Samaj, inspired by Rammohun Roy. For Tagore, Roy, whose vision of a whole and holy society, represented the most important revolutionary in India.[54] Roy's life and teachings encompassed a wide range of social and religious reform. He founded a religious organization "to teach and to practice the worship of the one God," based on his interpretation of Hindu scriptures.[55] Ultimately, Roy became "the most influential, rational movement of religious and social reform in 19th- century India"[56] and is frequently referred to as "The Father of Modern India."[57] Through much of his life, Tagore lectured on Roy and his work.

Foundational to the Brahmo Samaj, also known as Brahmoism or the Brahmo community, are the beliefs in one eternal God, and that no one needs an external emissary to have a relationship with

God. The Tagore family heritage with the Brahmo Samaj conflicted with liberal and conservative alike.[58] Tagore did not deny the role and importance of the pantheon of Hindu deities, and he sought life lessons from the ancient Hindu scriptures; he refused, however, to idolize any of the beings or texts. Symbolically and metaphorically, many of them pointed to God, but they neither represented nor encompassed God.

Tagore sought, for most his eight decades, to encourage people from all backgrounds and walks of life to search for holiness within themselves and within others. Humankind's "prime strength is in religion. [Humankind's] prime humanity is spiritual . . . The realization that we are a part of the eternal, that we are not just scattered little beings, is what makes for spirituality."[59]

Unquestioned loyalty to established ritual and dogma frequently blinds a spiritual seeker from recognizing the holiness, the God-ness, of another.

> Leave this chanting and singing and telling of beads! Whom dost thou worship in this lonely dark corner of a temple with doors all shut? Open thine eyes and see thy God is not before thee!
> He is there where the tiller is tilling the hard ground and where the pathmaker is breaking stones. He is with them in sun and in shower, and his garment is covered with dust. Put off thy holy mantle and even like him come down on the dusty soil!
> Deliverance? Where is this deliverance to be found? Our master himself has joyfully taken upon him the bonds of creation; he is bound with us all for ever (sic).
> Come out of thy meditations and leave aside thy flowers and incense! What harm is there if thy clothes become tattered and stained?

> Meet him and stand by him in toil and in sweat of thy brow.
>
> —Tagore[60]

Tagore beseeched his readers to "Open thine eyes and see thy God is not before thee" when one's ritual religious practices take precedence over the struggling and suffering of others. Tagore balanced his life-long spiritual practice of daily meditation and prayer with attention and intention to aid his sister and brother Indians, regardless of their backgrounds. His schools, his writings, his travels and lectures unfailingly emphasized that our holiest duty is to care for one another.[61]

I especially love this poem of Tagore's. It seems to echo the words of my primary spiritual teacher, Jesus of Nazareth, who summarized the entire corpus of Jewish law and teachings. "'Hear, O Israel: the Lord our God is one; you shall love the Lord your God with all your heart, and with all your soul, and with all your mind, and with all your strength'... [and] 'You shall love your neighbor as yourself.' There is no other commandment greater than these.'"[62]

What grieves me immensely is how persons sometimes declare that their way of worship is the only way, and that a holy life and relationship with God are impossible in any other tradition. This tunnel vision has caused the sufferings and deaths of untold numbers of people throughout human history. So many of the world's spiritual teachers, from various traditions, have exemplified and taught the unity of God and the sacredness of all beings.

Whatever one's spiritual background or practices, a person who seeks to welcome and embrace the God-ness in others opens her heart to the window of God's soul. The brokenhearted citizens of the world weep for that message.

In his seventh decade, Tagore gratefully accepted an invitation to visit Persia and was welcomed by the ruler and by the (Muslim) people. He spent a week at the home of Hafiz and spoke to enthusiastic crowds about their response to God's call of love. After spending a day in a Bedouin encampment in the desert, he recorded in his diary that his own privileged life was as far apart as could be from the illiterate Bedouin chief. The chief's words to Tagore about the prophet Mohammed really touched Tagore. "Our Prophet has said that a true Muslim is he by whose words and deeds not the least of his brother-men may ever come to any harm." Tagore noted, "I was startled into recognizing in his words the voice of essential humanity."[63]

I think Tagore, Jesus, the Buddha, Hafiz, and countless other misunderstood heralds of Truth whisper to us during our prayers and rituals. "Remember, Dear Ones, that heaven is a massive banquet whose guests include persons from every ethnic and spiritual heritage and every level of society, all sharing food and friendship and gratitude." When we listen to those urgings, we are all nourished, and God's prayers are answered.

53 Dutta & Robinson, 2009, p. 18
54 Tagore, 2006, p. 182
55 Basham, Ed., 2012, pp. 367–8
56 Dutta & Robinson, 2009, p. 28
57 Basham, Ed., 2012, p. 367
58 Kopf, 2011, pp. 299-303
59 Tagore, 2006, p. 92
60 Tagore, 1997a, #11, p. 27
61 Kopf, 2011, pp. 287-310
62 Mark 12:29–31, Revised Standard Version of Bible
63 Dutta & Robinson, 2009, pp. 316–7

The Weaker Sex?

> They dig by the river for bricklaying --- labourers
>   from the west country. Their little girl
> keeps scampering to the ghat. Such scrubbing
>   and scouring of pots and pans and dishes!
>   Comes running
> a hundred times a day, brass bangles jangling
>   clang clang against the brass plates she
>   cleans. So busy all day! Her little brother,
> bald, mud-daubed, not a stitch on his limbs, fol-
>   lows her like a pet, patiently sits
> on the high bank, as Big Sister commands.
> Plates against her left side, a full pitcher on her
>   head, the girl goes back, the child's hand in
>   her right hand. A surrogate of her mother,
> bent under her work-load, such a wee Big Sister!
> —Tagore[64]

For much of the world's history, and even today in most of the world, women and girls have done most of the work. Tragically, their work of caring for children, gathering firewood, hauling water, making and washing clothes, planting and harvesting the crops, and tending the livestock is almost always overlooked, underestimated, and even belittled. This work, upon which entire civilizations rest, merits no salary, no vacation or sick leave, and no retirement benefits. Tagore frequently expressed deep sympathy and compassion for the girls and women.

> And one day I saw the same naked boy
> sitting on the ground, legs stretched on the dust,
> Big Sister at the ghat sat scrubbing a pot with
> clay, turning and turning it.
> A soft-haired kid was grazing near by, gently nibbling the grass of the river-bank.
> Suddenly the kid drew near, and looking at the lad's face, gave a few bleats.
> Startled, the boy trembled and burst into tears.
> Big Sister left her pot, came running down. Her brother on one side, the goat on the other, she consoled both, giving them equal attention. Sister to both children, animal and human, mediatrix, she knit them in mutual knowledge.
>
> —Tagore[65]

Tagore's compassion for girls and women shines in so many of his literary works as well as his social activism on their behalf. In 1910, Tagore's inclusion of girl students in his little school, Shantiniketan, was a radical move. Girls (and most boys) from poor villages never had the opportunity to learn how to read and write, or seldom even to interact with children from other villages. From very early ages, the girls carried water, and tended the animals, and assumed other household chores, as reflected in the two Tagore poems above.

To his great sorrow, Rabindranath could not continue to educate girls at the school after a failed romance between two students ended in a suicide.[66] Before her death, his wife Mrinalini functioned as the surrogate mother for all the children at the residential school. Rabindranath said of her, "I can give [all the children at the school] everything but not a mother's love and care."[67] By the 1920s, Shantiniketan once again welcomed female students.

Hardly a day passes that I don't experience gratitude and humility for the rich educational opportunities of my life. The pain and grief I traversed during my first marriage and subsequent divorce felt like the end of the world at the time. What I know for certain is that

I might have survived physically, but not spiritually, had I remained in that relationship.

I am equally certain that my formal education would have ended had I remained in that marriage. My ex-husband, though intelligent and highly creative, spent his life beating himself up for not being perfect. When his grades in some favorite college classes did not meet his impossible standards, he dropped out, only a few credits shy of completing requirements for his bachelor's degree. He never returned. My desire to pursue additional schooling beyond my two bachelor's degrees threatened him. The marriage was a disaster for many reasons, not just because I wanted more schooling.

Shortly after my divorce, I summoned the courage to speak with a faculty member at the nearby graduate theological seminary. I dreamed of pursuing a graduate degree in music; that other thing always nipped at my soul, though—that sense that God wanted me to pursue a career in Christian ministry. A friend encouraged me to consider taking a class or two at the seminary ten minutes' drive from my employment. My job needed folks to work flexible schedules, to accommodate evening and weekend events, so enrolling for a class seemed feasible.

After meeting one time with the seminary adviser, I enrolled as a full- time student. Generally, the decision to pursue a graduate theological degree follows considerable prayer, contemplation, and research. A one- hour consultation to make such a life-changing detour sounds ludicrous, except as I always tell folks who ask how I ended up in the ministry, "God has a sense of humor." Besides, it really wasn't a spontaneous decision. It had been percolating in my heart and brain for about fifteen years by that time.

What I most needed to pursue that calling was something so simple, seemingly insignificant, in 21st-century America. Tagore would have understood. I believed that I was an unworthy candidate to follow my passion, not because I wasn't smart enough, and not because I wasn't committed enough, but because I wasn't a male. In rapid succession, several people affirmed that my gender, and my life-experiences thus far, would enrich the seminary community and fortify my abilities to minister to others in the name of Christ.

A few years after I completed seminary, I spent an intense nine months as a chaplain intern in a large hospital, training to learn better pastoral care skills. The setting required hours every week of individual and group therapy, in which each of us interns suffered having salt poured into our bruised and broken souls.

About halfway through the training, I had to submit a paper describing how I thought I was doing and what I was learning. I began to read the paper to the small group of staff and other interns, but all I could do was sob uncontrollably.

My paper began with words something like, "I am a woman who. . ." From the beginning of my internship, I knew that the other interns in my group disapproved of women clergy. The pain and the isolation of the whole thing just stuck in my throat that day.

I realize now that I must give thanks for that entire hospital experience, as it initiated me into the numerous times I would later face gender discrimination during my career in the army. It wasn't because I was a woman officer in the army. The discrimination was because I was a woman who was a chaplain. Like the big sister in Tagore's poems, though I helped many frightened and lonely people find healing and compassion. I never thought of myself as a mediatrix. I think I'll add that to my resume.

[64] Tagore, 1995, p. 104
[65] Tagore, 1995, pp. 104–105
[66] Das Gupta, 2004, p. 27
[67] Deb, 2010, pp. 101–2

Unsung Song

The song I came here to sing remains unsung.
Today too
the tune is set,
but I have only the wish to sing. The tune doesn't
 flow out.
The words don't string along.
Only in my soul
is the song's anxiety for expression.
Today too
that flower has not blossomed forth; only a certain zephyr whispered by. I did not see His
 face.
I did not hear His voice. Just from time to time
I hear the sound of His footsteps.
The object of my quest goes back and forth, passing by my door.
All day long
I've only had my mat spread out.
The lamp in my room remains unlit.
How O how
shall I call Him in?
I'm here
in hope of receiving Him.
My hope
stays unrewarded.

—Tagore[68]

Not a day passes in rich countries where the citizens do not hear or read entreaties from various charitable organizations. Some of the organizations are worthwhile. Some are scams. It never ceases to astonish me that so many people in 21st-century America continue to remain oblivious to the massive needs throughout our own country and throughout the world.

Most of us have either become immune to the pleas of the outcast and oppressed, or we have determined that it's someone else's responsibility to save the children, save the rain forests, save the whales, and to save the world. Even despite our apathy or callousness, deep in our souls, most of us still recognize our stinginess for what it is and feel inadequate. I think part of what prevents us from stepping out more generously is fear that our hearts will be changed, and our lives will be changed, if we really let ourselves become vulnerable and come face to face with the injustices.

"The song I came here to sing remains unsung," laments Tagore in this poem. When he wrote this poem, Tagore recognized that he had a greater life-purpose than his accomplishments thus far. The proliferation of self- help literature and workshops featuring therapists and tools for discovering and nurturing one's best self, attests to the yearning of so many of us. We want to do better, and we want to be better.

Between 1996 and 1999, I required that several dozen senior leaders in the US Army take a guided tour of an excellent Holocaust museum in El Paso, Texas. Part of my responsibilities at that time included serving as ethics instructor at the army's premier training institution for senior noncommissioned officers, those who would soon assume the title and duties of Sergeant Major, a position of tremendous leadership and authority.

Before each field trip to the museum, I dedicated several class sessions to some of the historical facts about the Holocaust and to exploring the reasons and underlying emotions that create mass bigotry. I coordinated with the museum to have a retired US Soldier as our tour guide and lecturer. He had served in Europe during World War II and had participated in the rescue of survivors of some of the Nazi death camps. Our tour guide said that he frequently spoke to school-aged children, whose teachers did not even have a basic understanding of the Holocaust.

Questions and comments he fielded each week ranged from horror to cynicism to outright denial.

I have long believed that ignoring the Holocaust guarantees future occurrences of apathy and genocide. We continue to witness multiple governments who tyrannize and slaughter their own citizens.

The history of the United States is also soaked with innocent blood. The Black Lives Matter movement has elevated racial prejudice in this country and worldwide. Other notorious victimizations include the Native Americans, the Japanese-Americans during World War II, the Chinese workers whose lives were sacrificed that we might have a transcontinental railroad, and the kidnapping and enslavement of millions of Africans.

I lived in Germany for two years at the turn of the 21st century. Sixty- plus years after the willful annihilation of millions of innocent people— Jews, gypsies, homosexuals, and persons with disabilities— the subject of the Holocaust was understandably difficult.

One of the great privileges of my time in Germany was participating in a reunion event for two groups of enemy soldiers from World War II: the American bomber pilots, and members of the German antiaircraft artillery. Decades earlier, their main goal in life was to kill each other. Along with these men, most of whom were then octogenarians, others in attendance at the reunion included those who were merely citizens of the German city the Americans targeted. That city, Schweinfurt, where I was stationed, housed a critical ball-bearing factory that was a prime target for destruction. Family members from both sides of the ocean, as well as German officials, other dignitaries, and Catholic and Protestant clergy also participated in the events. I believe this was their tenth annual reunion, alternating locations between Germany and the United States. About a hundred people gathered in 2001 to worship with each other, share meals, and to tell their stories. Translators assisted with written and oral accounts. The environment of friendship, forgiveness, and hope was extraordinary!

Despite the shining light of that reunion, I feel so distressed about the future of our world. The signs of prejudice and injustice, like blaring sirens and flashing red lights, defy incognizance. Anti-Semitic, Islamophobic, homophobic, misogyny, anti-disability, and anti-aging messages are all prevalent, popular fodder for comics, nightclubs, rap music, videos, television, movies, and other graphic arts. The same fear, hatred, and bitterness that fomented the world during the 1930s and 1940s continue to bubble into a lethal brew that could produce the world's final poisonous draught.

Of all the messages Tagore brought to the world, the "song" he adopted as his life's call related to how people from different cultures and backgrounds must respect and learn from one another. He tailored his message to encourage Asians, and Indians in particular, to acknowledge the gifts of the West, but without sacrificing the heritage and gifts from the East. "No one nation today can progress, if the others are left outside its boundaries."[69]

Tagore carried his perpetual message of goodwill and understanding and respect throughout the world, during times of peace and times of war. His message remains the clarion call for today's battered and broken world.

"I did not see His face,/ I did not hear His voice./ Just from time to time/ I hear the sound of His footsteps. . . How O how/ shall I call Him in?" the poet pleads. How indeed?

[68] Tagore, 2002b, p. 59
[69] Kripalani, 2008, p. 360

The Impossible Dream

In previous generations, the Tagore name implied wealth, but by the time Rabindranath attained adulthood, little remained of the family fortune. In 1901, Tagore transformed a couple of buildings on some rural land into a school. Rabindranath's father had bought the land years earlier to create a spiritual retreat center, and Devendranath bequeathed the land to his son. To start the school, Tagore had to sell almost everything he owned, including many of his precious books. To support her husband's school, his wife Mrinalini gave the only items of wealth she had ever owned—the jewelry that she brought into the marriage. Initially, the school comprised five teachers, three of whom were Christian, and five boys, one of whom was Tagore's own son.[70]

Despite unceasing financial challenges, Tagore refused to charge tuition for several years, consonant with his ideal that all children deserved an education. The school became known as Santiniketan (*Shantiniketan*), which translates "abode of peace." Tagore loved the children and his faculty members, but keeping the school solvent, and trying to assuage his many detractors who disapproved of his unorthodox methods took a tremendous toll on the poet. The British government even issued secret circulars warning parents against sending their children to Tagore's school. "The growth of this school was the growth of my life and not that of a mere carrying out of any doctrine."[71]

By the 1920s, the school had expanded to include a college with centers for Indian, Chinese, Tibetan, and Japanese cultures. After his worldwide travels, stimulated by Tagore's Nobel Prize in 1913, he became more convinced than ever that the hope of the world rested in communication and dialogue between eastern and western cultures. He saw firsthand the destruction of World War I, and he pleaded with leaders of his own country and other countries around the world, including the United States, for a spirit of cooperation and trust, rather than isolationism and fear. Tagore named his expanded school Visva-Bharati, from a Sanskrit text, meaning "where the world makes its home in a single nest."[72]

In addition to the academic and cultural presence of Visva-Bharati, Tagore facilitated another radical innovation. He had understood for years that the impoverished villagers surrounding the school needed more than the "three Rs." They needed to know how to build their own water wells, and how to recycle human and animal waste, and how to take better care of their lands so the crops would continue to grow. And they needed some basic healthcare. He also wanted to restore, at least to a couple of villages, traditions of music and epic readings from the ancient Indian history.

I endeavored all the time I was in the country to get to know it down to the smallest detail. . . I was filled with eagerness to understand the villagers' daily routine and the varied pageant of their lives. I, the town-bred, had been received into the lap of rural loveliness and I began joyfully to satisfy my curiosity. Gradually the sorrow and poverty of the villagers became clear to me, and I began to grow restless to do something about it.[73]

Thus began Tagore's institute of rural reconstruction called Sriniketan. Economists, agriculturalists, social workers, healthcare workers, and other industry and education specialists brainstormed the problems plaguing the villagers.[74]

The Indian bard dared to dream something so big that it seemed inconceivable. His schools, his life-saving work with the neighboring villages, and his outreach to the entire world began with a few simple poems. Like many of us who might nurture expansive ideals, Tagore suffered criticism and unending difficulties. How easy it is for us to relent, to let our own negative self-talk, or others' unflattering opinions, grind our visions into dust.

I am my worst critic, and heeding that condescending voice has doomed many ideas and projects. One of the losses that afflict many of us is the loss of our dreams, and I think we feel ashamed even to admit that. It must have been my fault anyway: I didn't deserve it, I wasn't good enough, or smart enough, or. . .and on it goes.

> An oldish man from India's north, skinny and tall.
> White moustache, shaved chin, face like a shriveled fruit.
> Chintz shirt. Dhoti in wrestler-style.
> Umbrella on left shoulder. Short stick in right hand. . .
> The wayfarer appeared
> on the outermost line of my universe, where insubstantial shadow-pictures move. I just knew him to be a person.
> He had no name, no identity, no pain, No need whatsoever of anything. . .
> He saw me too
> on the last limits of his world's waste land, where, within a blue fog,
> connections between men there were none, where I was – just a person.
> At home he has a calf, a myna in a cage,
> a wife, who grinds wheat between stones, fat brass bangles on her wrists.
> He has his neighbours . . . He has his debts . . .
> But nowhere in that world of his is there me – a person.
>
> —Tagore[75]

I suspect that many of us cling to the lies that we are not enough and should not pursue our heartfelt goals because we are afraid of each other. And we fear letting others know our true selves. Maybe that explains the popularity of reality shows. We crave knowing if others also hide in plain sight. Is there anywhere in her world or his world a place for me—a person? Likewise, is there anywhere in my world for that other one? Just think what we could do if we felt safe enough to entrust our dreams with each other.

[70] Kripalani, 2008, pp. 204–7
[71] Das Gupta, 2004, p. 25
[72] Das Gupta, 2004, pp. 66–72
[73] Das Gupta, 2004, p. 33
[74] Das Gupta, 2013, pp. 91–102
[75] Tagore, 1995, pp. 169–70

Mother And Daughter

"Every difficulty slurred over will be a ghost to disturb your repose later on."
—Rabindranath Tagore

So many ghosts may be waiting to haunt me! My relationship with my mother during the last three years of her life has been haunting me for a while now.

She died in the fall of 1999. My husband and I had moved her in 1996 from her home in Arkansas to an assisted living facility in El Paso, Texas, where we were living at the time. When Daddy died in 1995, Momma's health, which had been fragile to desperate for years, finally lost its fight. By the time my sisters and I decided we had to get Momma to a safer environment near one of us, Momma could barely walk, even with her walker. A sainted couple from Momma's and Daddy's church provided her with transportation, meals, and fellowship; Momma always put on a brave front around everyone else, so most people had no idea how little she was actually able to do on her own. Furthermore, she refused to consider letting us hire a live-in assistant. She also shunned any consideration of an assisted living facility in the little community where she had lived for the last several years.

I think Momma finally forgave us for moving her. Eventually, she realized what a relief it was to not have to prepare her own meals and manage all of her housework, and she enjoyed the companionship of other people day-to-day. Momma had always been so particular about cleanliness, so it must have grieved her that she could no longer bathe herself or wash her hair without help.

My husband and I had full-time jobs and a home that was not wheelchair-friendly. I should have given up my career to move her in with us, but even then, I knew that I would regret that decision and resent Momma for her part in it. As it was, I grew to resent her for how much it seemed to me that she took me for granted. One day in a multidisciplinary staff meeting at one of the facilities that housed my mother, I started weeping as the staff discussed Momma's care. They were so kind to me; they said mother and daughter relationships, especially with the eldest daughter, were often fraught with hazards.

Before Wayne and I moved Momma near us, I fantasized about how she and I would grow closer and enjoy cozy lunches and special afternoon outings. I did a lot of things with her and for her, but I just felt like her own personal staff assistant—I felt like her servant. What was so odd was that when I would walk into the facility where she lived, people would tell me how much she bragged about me and how glad she was to be near me. I never heard any of that from her or felt that she was proud of me.

When she died, after a long struggle with lupus and multiple complications, I felt immense sadness, but not just about the fact and the way that she had died. I also felt immense relief. No one should have to suffer that much. The word "lupus" means "wolf," because the disease is like a wild animal slowly tearing away and eating its victim. I was relieved that Momma was no longer suffering; I was relieved that I no longer had so much responsibility for her. I was relieved, because I thought maybe now that she was at peace, I could love her better.

Did I do enough for her? I don't know, but it was all I could do at the time. I wish I had been kinder to her sometimes. I wish she had been kinder to me sometimes. Forgiveness, love, regrets, sorrow, dreams— these comprise all of the main ingredients for a life. "Every difficulty slurred over will be a ghost to disturb your repose later on," Tagore predicted.

Not long ago, I had the only dream I can remember having about my mother. She was whole and healthy and smiling, nothing like the broken woman I bade good-bye to in the hospital bed years ago. She spoke no words, but gave me a huge bouquet of lavender. I think the previous difficulties between Momma and me have transformed from haunting ghosts into angels.

Getting To Know You

During my career in the army, I volunteered one time to teach a class about the basics of Islam. Since I had taken several graduate-level courses in Islamic studies at one of the leading universities in the nation, I felt qualified for the task. The setting for the class was a week-long training/worship retreat for Christian women from various military communities. I did not expect the committee to approve my proposal. I was surprised when the planning committee welcomed my presentation.

I spent several hours working on the class and preparing handouts. When I arrived at the retreat location, I was stunned to learn of numerous divisive conversations among the organization's officers and other senior chaplains. Of the ten or twelve folks in charge, at least one thought I should present the training session. I am told that about midnight before I was to teach my class the next morning, my lone supporter agreed to cancel my class, not because he thought it unimportant or irrelevant, but because he was concerned that things might get ugly if I proceeded. To say that I was devastated is an understatement.

The next morning in a large opening assembly/worship event, my advocate announced to several hundred women that the class was cancelled. The senior chaplain said some very kind things about me and my ability to teach this class. Then he offered a gentle and compassionate prayer. I had intentionally sat in the very back row, and I ran out of the room, blinded by my tears. I felt grateful and somewhat comforted when a couple of women dared to tell me that they were saddened to miss my class. My grief about this incident literally took my voice away for a couple of days. I had not been hoarse or sick. Then I could not speak above a whisper.

Healing

One of my favorite stories about Tagore relates to his activities to further positive relationships among Indians, regardless of their ethnic or religious heritage. The British viceroy of Bengal, Lord Curzon, ordered that October 16, 1905, would mark the official division of Bengal, generally delineated by populations of Hindus and Muslims. While thousands of Bengalis marched in the streets in protest, Tagore modeled cooperation and respect by adapting an ancient Hindu ritual. Sisters historically tied a piece of colored silk thread, a *rakhi* ribbon, on the wrists of their brothers to affirm their undying love. In front of many stunned onlookers, Tagore marched into a local stable and tied sacred Hindu *rakhi* ribbons around the wrists of several Muslims who cared for the horses and mules. The other Hindus feared reprisals or violence, but the peace- offering induced harmony. After that, Tagore led his parade into the main Muslim mosque and tied ribbons on the wrists of the mullahs. Everyone was smiling that day.[76] I wish someone had offered me a *rakhi* ribbon at that women's conference.

[76] Dutta & Robinson, 2009, pp. 144–5

Poop, Poverty, And Plague

It was my fault, not his. We adopted him a few months ago, and the folks at the agency were thrilled that we offered a loving home to a nine year old. Last evening, he was sleeping so peacefully that I didn't wake him, so he didn't go to the bathroom before we went to bed. This morning, I smelled it before I saw it. He apparently could not get me to wake up in time to let him outside, so he pooped on the basement floor. Buddy is a tricolor, seventy-pound coonhound with big brown eyes, a tail that wags his body, and the soul of sweetness. He makes some large piles of serious stink. Cleaning it up does not blend well with my morning cup of hot tea. But it caused me to think about so many privileges in my life.

My husband and I live in a lovely home in a safe, pleasant neighborhood. We have plenty of clean water that I do not have to walk miles every day to fetch. The floors in our home are made of ceramic tiles and wood, surfaces easily scrubbed and deodorized. Floors made of dirt and straw absorb urine and feces, and the stink stays. For all their faults, plastic bags contain gooey, smelly messes much better than paper or a handful of leaves. I tied up and disposed of the nastiness in our plastic, lidded garbage can. Since today was our weekly garbage pick-up, the whole thing was out of mind, sight, and smell in no time. Then I washed my hands thoroughly with antibacterial soap and water from our designer faucet. No longer did I need to devote to worrying about germs or disease or contamination of our drinking water from my unexpected morning chore.

In so many parts of the world, even in the United States of America, millions of people do not have clean water, adequate plumbing, solid floors, or a sanitary way to dispose of their garbage and sewage. How easy it is to ignore, belittle, or disregard persons who subsist in cardboard shacks, or garbage dumps, or lean-tos fashioned by a tree branch and a raggedy blanket.

In 1898, the plague reached Calcutta, after having caused untold suffering and death for a full year. Tagore cooperated with an American woman missionary to help combat the disease by collecting dead rats.[77] During Tagore's lifetime, massive famines and related diseases affected millions of people throughout India. Between 1869 and 1900, more than ten million Indians died because of a series of famines.[78]

Throughout Tagore's lifetime and still today, millions of India's citizens live in poverty unimaginable to most of us. In 1930, Tagore told an audience in Geneva that 80 percent of India's population suffered a chronic state of famine, and only 5 percent of Indians were literate.[79]

I feel overwhelmed and mournful by the amount of suffering in the world. So many people in our culture are "news junkies," and yet the empathy response to people and situations beyond our shores, or even beyond our own neighborhoods or families, seems to be diminishing. Partly, it's because we are afraid of each other, or more accurately, we are afraid of letting another see our most vulnerable self. It seems easier to blame the victims than to acknowledge the pain of our world.

The day after Hurricane Sandy had decimated much of the northeastern shores, leaving a million or so people without power and water, and reducing thousands to homeless status, Wayne and I were at the hospital for his radiation treatment. The fear and uncertainty I felt about Wayne's status seemed almost inconsequential compared to the destruction and devastation portrayed on every television set. A man in the waiting room at the hospital complained loudly to those nearby that he was exhausted of hearing about the storm. Soon, his name rang over the public address system for him to move to the treatment room for his radiation. I was shocked. How could someone suffering from cancer feel such hostility and/or apathy towards others whose lives were suddenly shattered?

My journey with Wayne through all the uncertainties and suffering of cancer caused me to feel ultrasensitive to others' pain and sorrows. I could barely watch the news for several months, not because I did not care, but because I did not think I could open my heart to more pain. Perhaps, the insensitive man awaiting his radiation treatment suffered from the same condition as me. We all do that: find ways to excuse our heartlessness, because we don't think we can open our hearts wide enough to let in any more pain.

> You came to my door in the dawn and sang; it angered me to be awakened
> from sleep, and you went away unheeded. You came in the noon
> and asked for water; it vexed me in my work,
> and you were sent away with reproaches. You came in the evening with your flaming torches.
> You seemed to me like a terror and I shut my door.
> Now in the midnight I sit alone in my lampless room and call you back whom I turned away in insult.
>
> —Tagore[80]

[77] Dutta & Robinson, Eds., 2005, p. 50
[78] Walsh, 2007, pp. 144–5
[79] Tagore2006, p. 345
[80] Tagore, 2011a, Vol. 1, #16 in "Crossing," p. 223

The Power Of One

A wooded trail where I frequently walk lies strewn with dozens of giant oak trees on the ground. Chainsaws and human greed had nothing to do with this destruction. We had so much rain this last spring that the ground was positively spongy, and the towering trees just toppled like bowling pins because their roots are so shallow.

What a metaphor for life. We may look strong, maintaining that appearance for decades. Then one day something as small as one too many raindrops knocks us to the ground. Likewise, entire societies can experience a tremendous shock by an event that at first seems unimportant.

In 1955, a petite, forty-two-year-old African American woman boarded a bus to go home after a long day's work at a local department store. The rules of the American South at that time demanded that African Americans always subjugate themselves to white people. Rosa Parks was tired of walking to and from multiple bus stops every day, tired of working her fingers to the bone for almost no pay, tired of not being able to use a public restroom or water fountain or get a decent education, and tired of being invisible. So as unassuming as a single raindrop or a gentle gust of wind, she refused to give up her seat on the bus to a white person. She could have walked to the back of the bus, but her feet and back hurt, so she didn't move. And that little action helped changed the course of the entire nation and would help topple a massive forest of racism and politically sanctioned bigotry.[81]

More than three decades earlier, what began as a holiday celebration became one of the galvanizing events for India. April 13, 1919, welcomed the official beginning of spring as one of the most significant days in the Punjabi year. Sikh and Hindu celebrants, dressed in their festive yellow turbans, blouses, and saris, crowded the city of Amritsar. The day before, the British authorities had declared martial law in the Punjab, following civil unrest because of the Montagu-Chelmsford reforms, which legalized prejudicial treatment against the Sikhs and all non-British Indians.

During the celebration, two British senior-ranking officers ordered their cavalry soldiers to herd hundreds of people into a park-like garden (*bagh*) area. The space, though open at the entry, was enclosed by high walls. The soldiers blocked the entrance and began firing at point-blank range, slaughtering 379 people, and maiming and injuring over a thousand more. The Hindu and Sikh men, women, and children could not escape, and an innocent celebration became a bloodbath that would change the course of history in India. In the months following, legalized brutality claimed 1,200 more deaths, 3,600 wounded, 258 public floggings, and countless other cruel and humiliating punishments.[82]

Tagore lived 1,300 miles from Amritsar, decades before the days of instant news coverage. When the stories about the massacre started spreading throughout the continent, fear and outrage gripped all of India.

One of Rabindranath's closest friends, C. F. Andrews, recounts being with Tagore when the news made it to Calcutta. "It will be impossible for me ever to forget the torture of his mind. Night after night was passed sleeplessly. At last, some relief came to him by renunciation of his knighthood as a protest against what had been done."[83]

The Indian poet renounced the incredible honor of British knighthood in a highly publicized letter to Lord Chelmsford. Tagore acknowledged that his action might make no difference, but it was all he could think to do to express solidarity with his beleaguered Indian sisters and brothers.[84]

When grief inspires courage, even if the action seems as insignificant as taking a seat on a bus, mailing a letter, or the weight of a single raindrop, sometimes a whole forest can fall.

81 Cain, 2012, pp. 1–2
82 Mansingh, 2000, Jallianwala Bagh Massacre, p. 201; Holroyde, 2007, Jallianwala Bagh, pp. 179–80
83 Tagore, 2002a, pp. 60–61
84 Dutta & Robinson, 2009, pp. 216–7

Castes

Tagore started his rural, residential school in southern Bengal, motivated by his own childhood frustration and anger at the accepted education methods. Rote learning, severe discipline, and inflexibility with schedules and pedagogy crushed the youngster's spirit. Freedom to question, explore, enjoy, and create became the hallmarks of Tagore's school, named Shantiniketan, a place of peace.[85]

The most shocking factor at Shantiniketan was that Tagore recruited students from different castes. One of the ancient rules of India required that upper-caste and lower-caste folks eat separately during mealtimes. When a visitor asked Tagore about the highest-caste Brahmin boys' expectations of segregation, Tagore replied, "Of course I could not force [the upper caste boys to eat separately] since freedom is the very principle of the school, it was not long before one by one they came and asked to be allowed to eat with the majority." [86]

When I visited India in 2008, some of the realities of a formal caste system smacked me like a fist in the face. Widowed women, young and old, were ostracized and disowned by their families. Lepers without fingers or feet resorted to lying on the streets and beg for their daily bread. Bands of gypsies survive abject poverty by teaching their children to cling to tourists like gum on a shoe. Impoverished villagers are sometimes forced out of their meager homes by upper-level caste members who don't want lower caste neighbors.

Like India, the United States continues to struggle with casteism, though we might not acknowledge it. Our caste system is like the emperor with no clothes, whom we would rather look away from and ignore the truth. Drug addicts, sex workers, ex-convicts, and child abusers fight at the bottom of our caste system. How these people ended up that way, and how our society might have assisted them to a more hopeful life are questions we would generally prefer not to ask.

Persons with familial or political or monetary influence almost always receive easier access to better schools, better jobs, and homes in safer neighborhoods. "Blue collar" refers to persons with often limited educational opportunities. Sometimes, the person does not have the financial or geographical ability to pursue additional schooling. Our society could not function without all the blue collar workers, such as factory workers, truck drivers, hospitality workers, mechanics, construction workers, and sanitation workers. We don't refer to that as a level of caste, but is it so different?

Someone born into an American caste, the son of a coal miner for example, can conceivably escape the dangers and drudgery of living and working underground most of his life. Unfortunately, the difficulties of securing the education and financial stability to move into a different career field seem as unlikely for most as the sun's shining half a mile down into the mine shafts.

Unlike so many Indians of the early 20th century, Tagore saw formal castes as an evil, which could and should be eliminated. The unbreakable rules of who, how, and when persons could interact with each other defied the possibility of learning from each other and of acknowledging the innate sacredness of every person. Tagore's opinions on this met with significant rivalry, especially from other members of his own caste, Brahmins. The orthodox Brahmins, from which Rabindranath's ancestors had been outcaste generations earlier, held incomparable influence throughout every level of society. In many parts of India, that is still the case today.[87]

Tagore grieved about the seemingly hopeless situation of the millions of persons labeled as "untouchable." He and his friend Gandhi disagreed about many things regarding the best direction for India, but they agreed that the plight of those condemned to the lowest caste must no longer be ignored or justified.[88]

> All manner of humiliation and disabilities from which any class in India suffers should be removed by heroic efforts and self-sacrifice.

Whoever of us fails in this time of grave crisis to try his utmost to avert the calamity facing India would be held responsible for one of the saddest tragedies that could happen to us and to the world.[89]

In the 21st century, the United States continues to separate people into classes and castes. Despite the hopeful and inspiring things about the United States, in many ways, we continue to be a broken nation.

85 Das Gupta, 2013, pp. 63–71
86 Das Gupta, 2013, p. 69
87 Holroyde, 2007, "Caste," pp. 76–79
88 Tagore, 2006, pp. 239–52
89 Tagore, 2006, p. 247
90 Pandey, 2013

Forgiveness

> I came out alone on my way to my tryst. But who is this that follows me in the silent dark?
> I move aside to avoid his presence but I escape him not.
> He makes the dust rise from the earth with his swagger; he adds his loud voice to every word that I utter.
> He is my own little self, my lord, he knows no shame; but I am ashamed to come to thy door in his company.
>
> —Tagore[91]

For many years of my life, I have recited the Lord's Prayer, or at least I listened while persons around me recited it. Several of the phrases in that prayer confuse and conflict me, but one in particular haunts me: "Forgive us our sins, as we forgive those who sin against us."[92] I am asking God to forgive me in the same measure as I forgive others. It is a humbling thought. Sometimes, I can forgive another who has hurt me or wronged me, but sometimes I would rather nurture my feelings of ill will, hop-ing that the irritant will magically transform into a pearl. If I refuse to forgive another, I somehow feel powerful, and I can inflict upon someone else the pain that another has caused me. I know that cherishing hurt feelings and wishing revenge on another cause my soul to bleed, but I do it anyway.

Tagore names the ego "my own little self." My ego shadows my every thought and action, and her hubris and insensitivity try to smother the holy spark that God birthed in my soul. My own little self loves to belittle another to try to improve my own status. My own little self thinks I deserve forgiveness, but I am often reticent to share that gift with one who has hurt me.

So many of us live in such an ongoing fog of envy and spite and resentment that we should be surprised that the crime rate does not surpass the population rate. And yet, millions upon millions of people worldwide recite that pesky phrase in the "Lord's Prayer" every day: "…forgive us our sins as we forgive those who sin against us." We don't really think about what that means, or if we do, we hope that God doesn't take this phrase literally! When I refuse to forgive another as well as when I refuse to forgive myself, I inhale poison with every breath. The reasons why one might choose to nurture resentment instead of forgiveness might seem logical and sensible, but refusing to forgive is just another way to smash one's own heart.

First, forgiveness is a choice one makes with one's mind. Forgiveness seldom happens if one waits until she feels like offering it. Whether the offence, or perceived offence, is being cut off in traffic, or long-term abuse, the wounded one frequently claims justification for anger and retribution. And here's the key: forgiving another may or may not free the perpetrator, but it always frees the wounded one. In the same collection of Tagore poems that included the citation about "my own little self . . . ashamed to come to [God's] door in his company," Tagore placed another poem that speaks to me about forgiveness.

> "Prisoner, tell me who was it that wrought this unbreakable chain?"
> "It was I," said the prisoner . . . "I thought my invincible power would hold the world captive leaving me in a freedom undisturbed. . . When at last the work was done, and the links were complete and unbreakable, I found that it held me in its grip."
> —Tagore[93]

Holding on to and strengthening resentment may not seem like grief, but it is. Nurturing resentment frequently masquerades as well-deserved anger, announcing itself to any who will listen. Buried deep within that cloud of darkness and hostility lie the remnants of a grief too painful, too vulnerable to acknowledge. The longer one cherishes the resentment, the more it consumes one's soul, like an ever-addictive drug.

"Forgiveness is giving up the hope of a different or better yesterday. . . Any memorized resentment of past events will limit and restrict our ability to participate fully in life."[94]

Tagore suffered numerous lashes against his soul. Similar events have fueled resentment and vengeance by many of us. His schools, his writings, his personality, and his theology buffeted attacks throughout his life. He grieved greatly each time he was misunderstood, misrepresented, and misled; he understood, though, that responding with anger and resentment were a slow form of suicide. Like anger and resentment, forgiveness builds over time—a process rather than an immediate conclusion. Tagore understood the poison of resentment, and he suffered the loneliness and exhaustion of choosing the path of forgiveness. [95]

Forgiveness, like grief, is hard work. When grief's primary fuel is anger, healing becomes almost impossible. After Jerry died, I had much about which I could be angry, but I took a mantra into my heart, and it saved my life. I knew with each day, and sometimes with each passing moment, I needed to make a conscious choice about my attitude. I could either get bitter or get better. I remain ever grateful that through that lengthy season of grief, my guardian angels and God knows who else, strengthened me enough for me to let go of much of the anger.

I continue to nurture resentments about so many things. If God takes to heart my prayer, to forgive me only as I forgive others, I'm in trouble.

[21] Tagore, 1997a, p. 46
[22] Matthew 6:12, Revised Standard Version of Bible
[23] Tagore, 1997a, p. 47
[24] James & Friedman, 2009, p. 138
[25] Bhattacharya, Ed., 1999, p. 98

Hold My Hand

When the weariness of the road is upon me, and the thirst of the sultry day; when the ghostly hours of the dusk throw their shadows across my life, then I cry not for your voice only, my friend, but for your touch.
There is an anguish in my heart for the burden of its riches not given to you.
Put out your hand through the night, let me hold it and fill it and keep it; let me feel its touch along the lengthening stretch of my loneliness.

—Tagore[96]

For the duration of Tagore's life, and continuing well into the 21st century, scholars have criticized Tagore's translations of his own poetry into English. The assaults claiming that Tagore should not have allowed the publication of his translations, wounded him and left him feeling vulnerable.

Perhaps part of Tagore's motivation for composing this song about his weariness and anguish lay in the ongoing challenges he faced with publishers and come-lately translators of his works. One of the difficulties for any artist, musician, author, or poet is exposing one's heart to complete strangers who may or may not treasure that gift. Many creative folks wither under the microscope of criticism. Tagore spent the rest of his life choosing, over and over, to seek peace instead of vengeance. He spent the rest of his life always choosing to remain vulnerable to even more criticism of his life's work, instead of just muting or hiding his creativity.

"There is an anguish in my heart for the burden of its riches not given to you," prayed the poet. "Put out your hand through the night, let me hold it . . . let me feel its touch along the lengthening stretch of my loneliness." Some people might equate these feelings of loneliness with lack of faith in the Divine. I feel the opposite. During those times in my life, when grief and anguish bubble to the top of my emotions like froth on a raging sea, I feel an emptiness that yearns for divine companionship formerly instinctual. My brain knows that God's gifts and graces surround me as surely as the oxygen I breathe; my heart, though, feels like a child who has lost her mother in a teeming public place.

Part of what haunts me about Tagore, in the best possible way, is his unflinching honesty about his spiritual quest. No whitewashing and no simplistic credos or formulas comprise Tagore's faith in God. Doubts, questions hard as nails, and naked grief anchor the poet's love of God. Many may find my identification with Tagore's faith journey puzzling or even heretical. Tagore's faith journey liberates and renews me.

Hundreds of times during the months prior to and following Wayne's cancer surgery, I would wake up in the night and reach over to check if Wayne was still breathing. During those long days while Wayne was too weak to get out of bed without help and attached to an IV pole for medicine and sustenance, I tried to manage daily affairs of our home and menagerie. Except for one four-day stay in the hospital several weeks before his surgery, and the fifteen days in the hospital following the surgery, Wayne was at home, and I cared for his every need. My life revolved around checking on him and nursing him, transporting him to medical appointments and emergency rooms, and caring for our four-legged family members. Exhausted and worried sick but hiding my fears from Wayne, I stumbled along, craving the least smidgen of encouragement like a drug.

We needed help from other people, but I found it painful to ask someone to bring me something nourishing to eat, or to call a friend to sit with Wayne so I could run an errand. Wayne expected to die, and the doctors were candid about the gravity of his condition. He almost died from the onslaught of simultaneous radiation and chemotherapy. Between the tumor in his esophagus and the multiple radiation treatments every week that burned his throat, he could not swallow anything including water for several weeks. He survived, barely, on frozen Gator Aid cubes.

One of the nurses announced that Wayne was at fault for his deteriorating condition. She claimed that if he had followed her instructions several weeks prior and gotten a feeding tube inserted, he would have avoided such bad shape. After she told us that, she walked out of the examining room, leaving us stunned and helpless. She did not return.

I have many nurses in my extended family, and I'm so proud of each one of them. I know they would be horrified to learn of that particular nurse's behavior. And I am grateful for all the healthcare providers who give of themselves selflessly. That one incident, though, was a bitter pill.

I helped Wayne get balanced with his walker, and we left to go to his chemotherapy infusion. After he was hooked up, I felt too anguished to stay in the room with him. I wandered around the treatment area so I could cry without Wayne's seeing me. A compassionate nurse calmed me down and helped us get home health services, enabling Wayne to receive fluids and nutrition through a tube at home. For at least a month prior to that, we had spent hours every single day traveling to hospitals and emergency rooms and waiting for him to receive a liter of saline solution. One liter per day, delivered slowly through an intravenous line, was as much stress as Wayne's heart could handle. No one can live for long on just one liter of saline solution per day.

The oncology doctors stopped the radiation and chemo protocols sooner than planned, because Wayne was too weak to continue. They had intended for Wayne's surgery to occur almost immediately after the last treatment. We knew, and the doctors knew, that Wayne could not possibly survive the surgery if they had proceeded right away. Several weeks later, a seven-hour surgery removed all the dead tumor, a third of Wayne's stomach, and most of his esophagus.

A couple of friends from church and my sister stayed with me in the waiting room. Almost eight hours after the surgery was over, we were still waiting to hear how Wayne was doing. The medical folks in post-op could not get Wayne's blood pressure and heart rate and pain stabilized enough to transport him one floor away to the ICU. Finally, a nurse escorted me back to the post-surgical recovery area. They don't usually let family members back there, but Wayne's nurse said she knew I was desperate to see my husband. Even as I write this, almost a year later, my eyes are flooding. My husband's whole body was quivering in pain, and he was crying out. Thankfully, he doesn't remember that. I will never forget it.

Prior to Wayne's surgery, the surgeon told us that the hospitalization time following this particular surgery is five to seven days. Nothing so far had gone as anticipated with his treatment. That did not change. Wayne did not leave the hospital for seventeen days. On the fourth or fifth day in the hospital, when we knew he was going to be there longer, my husband's spirit was broken. Several kinds of narcotic pain medicines offered precious little relief from excruciating pain. To create enough space in Wayne's body for the surgery, the doctor had to break one of his ribs and deflate one of his lungs. It was the week before Christmas, and we both felt depressed. I thought Wayne was going to give up fighting for his life. I did not know what else I could do to encourage him.

When the ghostly hours of the dusk throw their shadows across my life, then I cry not for your voice only, my Friend, but for your touch.

I called Wayne's supervisor at work. It was the Saturday before Christmas, and he was out shopping. I had only met this man once, but I knew that Wayne had high regard for him, and he kept checking on us by phone. Barely able to control my sobs, I called him and asked if he would please call Wayne and give him some encouragement. He drove straight to the hospital—no quick or easy trip in this giant metropolitan area—and spent over an hour with Wayne. He doesn't know it, but he might have saved Wayne's life. And I thank God for that sacred touch. The Heavenly Friend sent us many angels in human form throughout those months, and they saved both of us.

When the weariness of the road is upon me, and the thirst of the sultry day; when the ghostly hours of the dusk throw their shadows across my life, then I cry not for your voice only, my friend, but for your touch.

[96] Tagore, Vol. 1, 2011a, "Fruit Gathering," #59, p. 180

Many Worlds

My husband's health continues to concern us. His chronic hoarseness and nausea continue to worsen, almost a year after his cancer surgery. We anxiously await the results of the latest CT scan, because hoarseness and nausea predominated his symptoms as his cancer grew. Feeling stuck, I sought a certified hypnotherapist who could help me with a past-life regression.

The idea of reincarnation has seemed feasible to me for most of my life. From a very young age, I believed that my passion and abilities to make music were gifts to me from an earlier soul journey. For so much of my life, my music training and offerings focused on playing the piano. Over and over, people who heard me play told me that I expressed depth of feeling and intimacy when I played. Ironically, my shyness and introversion prevented my being able to share myself with people unless I was seated at the piano.

Tagore suffered similar fears of self-disclosure, relieved by writing poetry or dramas or painting. After I studied techniques of classical singing and grew into a vocal soloist, I received similar feedback that my singing touches people's spirits and offers them healing.

As a life-long, westernized Christian, the idea of reincarnation never appeared in any sermons or teachings I received in seminary; the possibility of reincarnation, though, always floated around in my brain, like a beautiful soap bubble that I could almost see but could not catch. All of the spiritual traditions that originated in India— Jainism, Hinduism, and Buddhism—hold reincarnation as a fundamental truth.[97] Tagore's life and culture were so infused with the assumption of reincarnation that I think he accepted it as a given. His **jeevan devata**, "God of Life," of whom he spoke so passionately and confidently affirm his belief in his ongoing soul's journey. When

I considered the idea of pursuing a past-life regression, I felt excited and relaxed about the possibilities.

Within my depths there is a vast and old "me" – which is my **jeevan devata** – who dwells in many realms and guides me in this one. . . .

In each one of us the **jeevan devata** tries to forge a rapport and union with the God of the Universe. . . . My **jeevan devata**, my companion in many worlds, is building for me a beautiful, eternal link of love as a bridge . . . with God.[98]

When I met Marybeth, and she embraced me, I felt so at ease and hopeful, despite losing my way and having to call for directions. I was in spitting distance to the address, and yet I couldn't find it—symbolic, perhaps, of this whole portion of my soul's journey. Part of me believes that I am whisper-close to something that eludes me, and part of me feels too frightened to continue.

Several years ago, when I first glimpsed the direction this work with Tagore would take me, I thought I would summarize some of my grief experiences and empathize with some of Tagore's grief experiences. The thing about real life, though, is that when you think you've learned your lessons and gained the wisdom you need. BAM! Like a superhero in distress, you get whacked as a powerful reminder that your journey is lightyears from completion.

Four days ago, after several weeks of anxiety, Wayne and I visited yet another medical specialist to receive the results of Wayne's latest CT scan. We tried to repress our fears that more cancer cells might lurk in his throat: an area unexamined for over a year. The ENT doctor treated us with dignity and compassion—and humor. Fully cognizant of the massive toll Wayne's cancer surgery took on both of us, the doctor listened to us, examined Wayne's throat and pronounced that "nothing in there will get him." Ever since, I seem to be a well overflowing with tears.

I am so grateful and yet ever weary and worried about my dear husband. Permanent nerve damage in his stomach creates an hour, or several hours, of pain and some nausea every time he eats. Permanent nerve damage in his vocal cords robs him of normal and painless speech. And, even harder on him, he can no longer sing. Like me,

Wayne is a musician who needs to make music as much as he needs to breathe. The nerve damage in his stomach and throat, and also in his back, are from the surgery that saved his life. Sometimes, as I watch him suffer most of the hours of every day, it feels like punishment for something I can't explain. My past-life regression offered me some insights as gentle and hopeful as a few twinkling stars in a dark sky.

After about forty-five minutes of induction into a trancelike state of altered consciousness, Marybeth asked me to describe a shape that would help anchor and heal me. At once, I sensed a spiral of light awaiting me. She encouraged me to find a time in my past when I felt safe and comfortable and successful.

"Look at your feet," she directed. "And your hands. And what are you wearing?"

My feet are small and unshod. My skin is light brown, my hair is long, dark, straight, and coarse. I am a young woman wearing some animal furs. My tribe of many dear people live in this canyon area, neighbored by a peaceful river. Dirt and rocks blanketed the beach, and a log fire offers warmth and protection. My name is Anais, and I feel safe and happy. The rough pebbles under my feet, the sound of the wind and the water, the sweetness of it all, embrace me. I feel so connected to everything.

I am holding my tiny baby whom I love more than my life. My happiness melts into tears as I realize my baby is dying. I want to die, too. I am certain that it's my fault my baby is dying. I can hardly bear the pain. I think I ate something that made me sick, and when my baby nursed, she got deathly ill. The meat didn't taste right when I ate it, but my hunger gnawed at me like a ferocious animal. All of us were starving; many others, besides me and my little girl, got sick.

My baby and I sleep awhile in our little cave, and when I wake up, she is limp. I yell for someone to help me, but no one knows what to do.

"What shape represents this, and where is it in your body?" Marybeth asks.

I have a hard, black ball stuck in my throat. "Use your spiral of light to dissolve that."

Now I feel free enough that I can describe the situation without collapsing in grief.

Fear of starving to death ruled our little community like a despot.

Marybeth asks me to localize the fear in my body. It's in my brain and blinding yellow. I can't stop thinking about how afraid and desperate I feel.

"What do you do to try to help your baby?" Marybeth asks.

I sing to her, and she relaxes into sleep. But after some time, she won't wake up. Everyone tries to comfort me, but I am bereft. So much sadness, dark as the darkest night. We have to find a place to bury her where the wild animals won't carry her off. We climb up onto one of the cliffs where friends and family dig a hole. I wrap her in furs and lay her tiny body there. Carefully, we cover my angel with big, heavy rocks to protect her. The outpouring of compassion from my tribe warms me like the log fire on the beach. "It's not your fault," they assure me. "We know how much you loved her. All of us were so hungry and desperate to eat something. All of us ate the bad meat to keep from starving to death."

Out of nowhere, a magnificent eagle soars overhead and drops a beautiful feather at my feet. I know that this is a sign that the eagle is going to take care of my baby's soul, and I feel so relieved. A few days later, I see the same eagle. He's resting on a high rock and seems to be watching me. I feel comforted.

"Put the feather somewhere in your being right now," Marybeth directs me, "and anchor it into your consciousness." After a few moments, she suggests that I search for another time and place that connects me to the fear.

Where am I? Who am I? My feet are protected by big boots made of animal furs. Snow as far as I can see, and bitter, blowing cold assault me. I am a man whose tribe literally threw me out here to die. My entire body trembles, frozen in fear.

Marybeth suggests that I put the fear inside an expanding balloon. Suddenly, the popping sound causes me to practically jump off the table where I lay. "You can release the fear now. You are safe. Breathe into your spiral shape."

I can remember that time now without terror, without desperation. My sense of vulnerability dissolves like a snowflake in the sunshine. I did not die out there, in the frigid isolation. I walked out of that lonely, terrifying space. I found a way out.

"That's wonderful," Marybeth affirms. "Fear has no power over your true self. What is happening now?"

I feel safe now that I have journeyed to a distant, wooded area brimming with sunshine and life. I take my boots off, because my feet are getting hot. The grass is magnificent, like a favorite blanket.

The people in my former village exiled me because I tried to protect some innocent women whom the council declared were evil. They burned the women. My terror and grief consumed me, like the flames engulfing the women. Try as I might, I could not stop this horror. My outrage guaranteed my punishment.

When I found courage inside the fear, the sun came out and showed me new life. I see a huge nest high up in the trees. It's my nest! I am Eagle, and whenever I want, I can fly up there and see all around. I feel so safe, and everything is so beautiful and grand. Gratitude and energy surround and infuse me.

Now that the terror is dissipated, I can describe the new life I created after being exiled into the snowstorm. I find another village where the people accept me as a person of wisdom and compassion. My gratitude and humility almost defy description as I live the rest of that lifetime surrounded by love and respect. After many years, I leave that plane, feeling whole and happy.

I tell Marybeth that my journey is complete. Two and a half hours reconnected me to three distinct lifetimes many thousands of years ago.

The primary insights I gained from my past-life regression filter into several categories: my relationships with other people, my relationships with nature and non-human beings, my sense of calling to offer music as healing, my constant struggle to keep fear from crippling me, and my recognition of the initiatory passages thus far in this lifetime.

As the young mother with the baby, I experienced immense love and tenderness from my clan. I only knew that time and place and

Healing

those people. The rules and rituals of life remained unchanged for many generations. How often I have thought how radically different my life would be had I lived in the same community my entire life. Loved and nurtured by some folks for decades, or resented and misunderstood by others for decades. If I lived and died in that forever place, those with whom I grew up, and my elders who watched me grow, might decide they know me so well that they can predict my thoughts and actions. Efforts to stretch my mind and pursue new interests may be ridiculed and belittled. The community that represented home might have become a prison.

Those who try to find a new way of being or thinking sometimes seem anathema, even suspect.

Throughout the history of the world, unknown multitudes of women and girls have been marginalized and suffered horrific deaths for something as innocuous as trying to heal a child with special herbs from the forest. Their only crimes were openness to new ideas and compassion. My experience as the horrified man who tried to advocate for and protect similar women caused me to experience the terror of unjust punishment. Like the "witches," I found myself in unimaginable danger from those I thought I knew and could trust.

For much of my current life, I have tried to advocate for those who might seem invisible, or "invalid" (in-valid). Those in human and non-human form whom others rejected and invalidated touch my soul.

When the family came into church today, the father held his son's hand to help steady the young man. His whole body twitched as he walked in a lopsided gait, while his smile shone wholeness. From my location, I could see the father and son standing shoulder to shoulder, face-to-face, during the singing of some upbeat praise hymns. At about half a head shorter than his dad, the mostly grown young man beamed as he and his father sang into each other's eyes and touched their heads together. I don't know this family, and I doubt that the young man can drive a car, calculate sales tax, or hold a traditional job. From my brief observation, I think that he knows better than most of us the meaning of life: to love and to be loved. For over eleven years, I worked with, and learned from, persons like this young man whose mind and body work differently from many of us. I learned more from these other-abled persons about theology and God than in seminary.

For twenty-four years, I worked with, and learned from, men and women in our United States military. Those with the least rank and privileges often described feeling ignored and underappreciated. I felt honored and humbled whenever someone trusted me with pain and sorrow.

For over twenty years, I have regularly sung in nursing homes, hospitals, and hospices, to folks who feel ignored and underappreciated. To hear their stories humbled me, to realize how rich and varied were their contributions; now their bodies and minds seem to have imprisoned them.

Recently, I have been singing at naturalization ceremonies, and I am awestruck by the tenacity and courage of millions upon millions of immigrants in this country.

I have learned so much from the other-abled folks, from the junior soldiers, from those challenged by their physical and mental health, and from so many others who have smacked into a wall of discrimination. I feel great sadness that our nation consigns so many people to invisibility.

As I reflect on my past-life regression experience, I recognize the pain of feeling invisible and powerless. Even in my privileged, highly educated status in this country, instances way too numerous to count have left me feeling ignored, invalidated, and underappreciated. Because of my own struggles and pain, I can be more effective and compassionate with those who need a friend or advocate. And I acknowledge the tremendous courage of those, like Tagore, who selflessly advocate for those who seem to have no voice. My experience as the man exiled because he cried out against injustices literally sent shivers down my spine. Fear of angering someone in authority, and fear of retribution for my actions, cripple me sometimes. Perhaps my chronic foot problems generate from my soul's journey and fear of standing up for what is right, rather than a malformed bone structure in this present incarnation.

Experiencing the brokenness of feeling rejected and outcast, and the wholeness of feeling loved and accepted, unite my regression journeys and my contemporary existence. The fear of that pendulum swing towards rejection frequently haunts me and prevents me from pursuing the noblest callings of my life.

How do I expand my vision and confidence to fully embrace my Eagle self? Powerful, fearless, imbued with and inspired by strength and beauty, Eagle sees no boundaries and relishes every tree and every breath of wind. Her approach to life models my goals and is mentored by so many spiritual leaders.

I feel that the highest commandment of all is that of sympathy for all sentient beings. Love is the foundation of all religion. Let me not bring sorrow into this world, let me spread happiness. Let me sympathize with the happiness, sorrow, and pain of all creatures so that I hurt none – that is true religion, and we should try to live up to this holy ideal.[99]

All the mistakes and struggles of my life to this point are my greatest teachers, and I try to give thanks for them. They function as my initiation into the next phase of my life as teacher about Tagore's wisdom through the cycles of grief.

In classic Vedic understanding, "I am that."[100] I am the oppressor and the oppressed. I am the one who experiences sorrow, and I am the one who causes sorrow. I am the one who exalts in joy and gratitude, and I am the one who ridicules joy and denies gratitude. I am sacred, and I am profane. I am music and poetry and drama and dance, and I am ugliness and bigotry and a wall to creativity. I am a conduit of hope and love, and I am a tunnel of despair and destruction. When I can acknowledge and embrace those parts of myself that are less than I seek to be, only then can I truly offer hope and healing to others whose souls are broken.

One of the things that I most admire about Tagore is his brutal honesty about his own struggles. And he lifts those struggles as offerings to God for transformation.

> When the heart is hard and parched up, come
> upon me with a shower of mercy
> When all grace goes into hiding, appear before
> me as the nectar of music

When work assumes a terrible form and closes in from all sides with a roar
Appear at the edge of life, with soft footsteps, O Saviour
Emptied of generosity when my impoverished mind lies in a corner Break open doors and appear before me in regal splendor, O Generous One
When desire blinds the mind in a dusty haze of delusion
O Pure One, O Wakeful One Appear in your brilliant radiance.

—Tagore[101]

[97] Campbell, 2003, p. 44
[98] Som, 2009, pp. 70–1
[99] Dutta & Robinson, Eds., 2005, p. 38
[100] Clothey, 2006, pp. 33–4
[101] Tagore, 2009, #45, p. 268

Linda L. George, Ph.D.

"Reflection on Tagore's poem and My Past-life Regression" by Linda George

When my heart is hard and parched up, like a man who fears the vengeance of angry and frightened neighbors,
Come upon me, Holy One, with a shower of mercy.
When all grace goes into hiding, like the grief and despair of a heart-broken young mother,
Whisper through me as the nectar of music singing a lullaby to her dying baby.
When work assumes a terrible form and closes in from all sides with a roar, like acquaintances who attack my character because I don't believe the same way they do,
Appear at the edge of my life, with soft footsteps, O Savior.
Emptied of generosity when my impoverished mind lies in a corner, like someone buried in frozen exile,
Break open doors and appear before me in regal splendor, O Generous One.
When desire blinds my mind in a dusty haze of delusion, like the urge to strike back at those who have hurt me,
O Pure One, O Wakeful One, appear in your brilliant radiance, like an eagle whose massive wings carry me into the sunlight.
O Pure One, O Wakeful One, carry me into your brilliant radiance that I might reflect you.

Burying One's Child

Several years ago, before becoming immersed in Tagore's work, I came across one of his poems while doing an online search. Like so many of his poems that are posted on the internet, there was no reference as to the origin of it.

> This song of mine will wind its music around you, my child, like the fond arms of love.
> This song of mine will touch your forehead like a kiss of blessing. When you are alone it will sit by your side and whisper in your ear, When you are in the crowd it will fence you about with aloofness.
> My song will be like a pair of wings to your dreams, it will transport your heart to the verge of the unknown.
> It will be like the faithful star overhead when dark night is over your road.
> My song will sit in the pupils of your eyes, and will carry your sight into the heart of things.
> And when my voice is silent in death, my song will speak in your living heart.
> —Tagore[102]

I tried unsuccessfully to locate the context of this poem. When and why and for whom did Tagore write this?

About four years later, as my collection of books by and about Tagore continued to grow, I found the poem at last. Tagore wrote it in 1903 as part of a collection of poems entitled Shishu, "The

Child." After his Nobel Prize, when the world clamored to hear more of his poetry, Rabinranath translated Shishu into English and named the collection *The Crescent Moon*.

Five months prior to the writing of this poem, Tagore's thirty-year-old wife died. She was under doctors' care, but they could not diagnose her symptoms. The couple's older son, Rathindranath, later recalled the last time he saw his mother. He said she could not speak as tears rolled down her cheeks.[103]

Middle daughter, Renuka, age eleven, had contracted tuberculosis shortly before her mother's death. After his wife, Mrinalina, died, Tagore left the fourteen-year-old Rathindranath with one of the male teachers at Shantiniketan. Then he took Renuka and six-year-old son Sami to a cabin in the mountains, hoping that the clean, crisp air might cure his little girl.[104]

While the family were in the mountains, Tagore wrote poems and stories for his confused and hurting children. This poem and many of the poems in *The Crescent Moon* were birthed at that time. "This song of mine" is especially heartbreaking when one realizes the context. The poet-father promised his children a song that will fill them with love and companionship and hope, even after his death. "When my voice is silenced in death, my song will speak in your living heart." Rabindranath was healthy, not dying, but his daughter was very ill. Why did he speak of his death at that time? What the children thought of this poem is not recorded anywhere, as far as I know. If either of the children understood that their father spoke of his own death so soon after having lost their mother, they must have been terrified.

I think this poem was Tagore's prayer that his daughter would recover and live a long life, eventually burying her father. He could not conceive of the idea that his child would die so young. A few months later, she died.[105]

Five years later, on the anniversary of his wife's death, Rabindranath's youngest son Sami died of cholera. He was only eleven, and his father was crushed.[106]

I cannot imagine the pain of burying one's child. That is a grief too deep for words.

[102] Tagore, 2011a, p. 153
[103] Dutta & Robinson, 2009, p. 137
[104] Dutta & Robinson, 2009, p. 138
[105] Dutta & Robinson, 2009, pp. 137–8
[106] Dutta & Robinson, 2009, p. 148

Seeing God

> I call her Krishnakali, my dark blossom, Though
> villagers call her the dark girl.
> On a cloudy day I had seen her in the field Had
> seen the dark girl with doe-like eyes! Her
> veil had fallen and her head was bare. Her
> tresses were swinging over her neck. Dark?
> No matter how dark she was to others, I had
> seen her beautiful doe-like eyes!
> Thick clouds had made darkness descend. Her
> dappled cows had lowed in dismay.
> Perplexed, this dark doe-eyed beauty Had rushed
> out from her hut anxiously. Peering intently
> at the sky,
> She had heard the thunder rumbling… Suddenly,
> the wind swept in from the east. The paddy
> fluttered playfully in the breeze.
> Standing by myself in a corner of the aisle,
> I saw her all alone in the middle of the field.
> Whether we had exchanged glances then,
> I guess no one will ever know besides us. Dark?
> No matter how dark she was to others, I had
> seen her beautiful doe-like eyes then!
> —Tagore[107]

So many of Tagore's poems and stories elevate girls and women to a status of dignity far surpassing that of their daily reality. The girl described in this poem is not unlike millions of girls in rural Indian villages, and rural villages in so many impoverished countries. Her workday never ends: responding to the needs of everyone in the household, gathering wood or dung for fuel, preparing bread and vegetables and cooking them over an open fire, toting heavy, splashing buckets of water from the river, doing the laundry by pounding on the clothes with rocks at the river's edge, and caring for young children and the family's precious farm animals. This girl's skin, darker than most of the villagers', caused her to be ridiculed and further degraded. The villagers did not know, or care to know, her name. They just called her "the dark girl."

Tagore wrote this poem in 1900 while he was living on the piece of land his father bequeathed him, trying to establish his school.[108] A few ramshackle buildings, some parched land, and lots of trees and wide-open sky would one day evolve into a university. For several years prior, Tagore had traveled on his houseboat, along the Padma River, taking care of his father's numerous estates. During this time, Rabindranath began to understand the hardships of typical Indian villagers. Always the keen observer, he often described persons in their daily ordinariness, recognizing a sacred spark that others missed.[109]

That analogy that no Indian would ever miss, but might not be recognized by 21st-century Americans, is the name Tagore offered this girl. "Krishnakali" combines the names of two of Hinduism's most powerful deities into one stunning revelation. Krishna, the hero of the Indian classic *Mahabharata*, commands widespread devotion as a personal God.[110] Krishna is India's most popular deity, whose incarnation is at once both human and divine.[111] The girl's dark skin reminded Tagore of the goddess Kali, also dark-skinned. Kali's manifestation bespeaks incredible strength, power, and destruction.[112]

Imagine comparing a waitress at the local bar, or the trash collector, or a homeless person on the street, to not just one, but two, of our most revered and famous figures—Abraham Lincoln and Mother Teresa. That will suggest the intensity and authority with which Tagore anointed this nameless, marginalized girl.

The other shocking implication of this poem peeks through in the lines: "Whether we exchanged glances then,/ I guess no one will ever know besides us." I think Tagore was referring to *darshan*, the privilege of seeing and being seen by one greatly exalted, especially a divine being. Tagore's repeated description of the girl's "beautiful doe-like eyes" echoes the fact that large, conspicuous eyes are striking in many Hindu divine images.[113] Whenever one visits any of the innumerable temples and sacred sites in India, the ultimate boon is to see and be seen by the deity.[114]

What I love about this poem is Tagore's acknowledgement of the sacredness of everyone. In India, as in many other eastern nations, placing one's "praying" hands in front of one's face, and bowing to another, signifies respect and honor. The action is called namaskar and asserts, "That which is sacred in me honors that which is sacred in you."

The union of the male and female—Krishna and Kali—recognizing that neither is complete without the other, is ubiquitous throughout India. Almost every male deity has a female partner. The word *kali* means black. "She is that which is beyond all imaging, that darkness, that mystery out of which all things come, and back into which they go."[115]

For a long time, I have grieved the almost exclusive masculine language and imagery about God in the Christian literature. I never considered God anything except masculine for decades. Now, I celebrate and explore the divine feminine and yearn for greater expression of that in sermons and hymnody. I am convinced that Jesus and much of the Judeo- Christian heritage originally embraced male and female aspects of divinity.

Despite what we seldom seem to hear in Christian communities, I am positive that Jesus had women disciples. When, for example, Jesus visited his dear friends Mary and her sister Martha in their home, Mary "sat at the Lord's feet and listened to what he was saying."[116] Kenneth E. Bailey, an acclaimed research professor of Middle Eastern New Testament studies, reminds us that sitting at the feet of a rabbi such as Jesus equates with being a disciple of that one. Mary's sister Martha, who seemed to be angry because Mary wasn't helping with the kitchen chores, "…is upset over the fact that her 'little sister' is seated with the men and has become a disciple of Rabbi Jesus."[117]

I am certain that Jesus encountered many dark-skinned girls taking care of their goats or cows, just like the girl Tagore named

Krishnakali. And, like Tagore, Jesus would have treated her with dignity and respect, and he would have seen the holy spark shining through her soul.

[107] Tagore, 2011b, "Krishnakali," 248–9
[108] Som, 2009, p. 257
[109] Tagore, 2008a
[110] Basham, Ed., 2012, p. 307
[111] Holroyde, 2007, "Krishna," p. 202
[112] Flood, 1996, pp. 177–8
[113] Eck, 1998, p. 7
[114] Eck, 1998, pp. 7-8
[115] Campbell, 2003, pp. 50–1
[116] Luke 10:39
[117] Bailey, 2008, p. 193

Searching For Home

Several hours before daylight, I woke up feeling strange and uneasy, and then I remembered an image from my dream. *What was that about?* I thought. And as sudden as a gasp, I started to panic. I knew what it was about. "Wayne, please wake up," I cried as I gently shook him. Neither of us ever sleeps well anymore, and I know how much he needed his sleep, but I had to talk to him, or I thought I would explode. As soon as he opened his eyes and asked me what was wrong, I started crying. Between sobs, I explained how overwhelmed I've been feeling, and that the latest news knocked the wind out of me.

On Friday afternoon, one of Wayne's numerous doctors called to say he had a cancellation and could perform Wayne's total shoulder replacement surgery three days from now. Wayne and I decided he should go ahead, moving his surgery up a whole month. My husband's shoulder had no cartilage, but he's had so many other health issues that the shoulder had to wait. I've nursed Wayne through two total knee replacements, plus his cancer surgery and an emergency open heart surgery, which he survived by a hair's breadth. The recoveries from each of these surgeries was grueling, and Wayne needed my help much of the time. My mind and body and spirit needed help too! I told myself I can handle this, while trying to complete my dissertation.

Ever since Wayne's cancer diagnosis twenty months ago, I've had less energy than a sloth in hibernation, so as usual, I went to bed early last evening. A few hours later, I jolted awake. My dream centered on one image from one scene in Ron Howard's docudrama film *Apollo 13*, about the failed lunar mission. After an explosion sent their rocket tumbling, the three astronauts knew they only had one chance to get back to Earth in their damaged craft. To compensate for the destroyed guidance systems, the crew worked to make the course corrections manually—something they weren't trained for. The ship lurched violently while the men burned some excess fuel, without benefit of a computer. Through the small window, one of the astronauts used the distant planet Earth as a reference point to align the craft's trajectory. Keeping Earth within that window was their only hope of survival.

The sight of the magnificent, yet distant Earth through a tiny window woke me up. Anxiety and fear threatened to suffocate me. What if Wayne dies during this next surgery? What if the surgery doesn't work, or makes his shoulder worse? Or he suffers even more permanent nerve damage, like in his cancer surgery? Will we ever be able to go back "home" to how our former lives were, to resume our favorite activities together, to feeling safe? Will Wayne ever again live without pain wracking his body every day, or will he ever be able to eat without the constant indigestion and nausea? What if something happens to me, and I can't take care of him? And will I ever complete my dissertation and receive the degree for which I have worked for years? I long to look through that window and see a beautiful life, not rollicking uncertainties and potential dangers. So, Wayne held me, and I sobbed. I felt bad that he felt bad because I felt bad.

The last few years of Tagore's life pummeled him with illness and pain. His was a remarkably long life, for his era and location. He remained engaged with the world, kept abreast of news, continued to write many letters every day, and penned poetry. In 1940, one year before his death at age eighty-one, the poet who loved science, and whose heart broke as he understood the inevitability of World War II, offered this testament to life from his sickbed.

> Under this vast universe pain's mill-wheel rotates,
> grinds planets and stars to powder.
> Sparks flash, scatter suffering on every side,
> ash-webs from annihilated worlds
> permeating in an instant...

> Every moment unfolds unending worth to con-
> sciousness invincible . . .
> Such enduring vigor . . .
> to find pain's limits –
> on a fevered, unnamed pilgrimage, together,
> from path to path,
> penetrating caves of fire, to find care's origins,
> provisions of unending love.
> —Tagore[118]

Throughout the history of humankind, persons from every path have traveled together "to find care's origins,/Provisions of unending love." The ultimate irony of love is that the more we open ourselves to love, the more we open ourselves to pain. And yet we keep searching and praying and crying for love. The hope of Home never ceases to amaze and astonish as we seek "provisions of unending love."

[118] Tagore, 2001, "Sickbed 5," pp. 5–6

Lessons From Tagore On Healing

A. NURTURE GRATITUDE

The adage to practice an attitude of gratitude is neither new nor unique to one person's teachings. All the world's major spiritual traditions encourage thanksgiving as a way of life. Nevertheless, it bears repeating that one can never give thanks too often, and that sincere gratitude heals the giver. Tagore's poems and songs and other writings abound with gratitude. The following song attests to the healing power of gratitude even when it seems counter-intuitive to feel grateful.

> My mind is unwilling to take account of just what I didn't get; Today a flute is playing the heart's light and shade.
> I have loved this earth, memories of that keep coming back,
> In so many springs with fresh flowers the south wind filled this very basket.
> The tears are there, hidden in the heart's deep, inaccessible layer, Where the essence of pain secretly brings fruition to endeavor.
> True, sometimes the strings broke, but about that who would mope. Still, again and again the note played, today that's what I recollect.
> —Tagore[119]

Just shy of his sixty-fourth birthday when he composed this, Tagore does not hint at the specifics of the pain he references, other than to indicate that it seemed to recur. "Sometimes the strings broke... Still, again and again the note played..." Over and over in his poetry, he speaks of himself as a musical instrument, as a flute or reed, and as a veena, a traditional stringed instrument of India.

When his heartstrings broke, Tagore reminded himself of the many previous incidents in which his life's notes continued to sing forth, despite pain and tears. He could give thanks for what he learned and who he became, allowing his memory to alchemize the pain into treasure.

B. EXPECT HOLINESS

> For those who feel deserted and have none else
>   You alone remain with Your affection
> For those unsheltered and lost
> There is place in Your abode, There is no companion but You
> As one faces the endless span of life... I know
>   that I will find You at all times Among people and across the ages
> In time and thereafter
> Until there remains no one, no earthly barrier between us.
>
> —Tagore[120]

This prayer-song of Tagore's echoes a recurring sentiment throughout his life: everyone is holy. I certainly don't always act like it, or remember our God-ness, and it is a message rejected by many. How much easier is it to blame "original sin" for everything wrong with the world? How much easier is it to demonize one whom I don't like, respect, or understand? How much easier is it to deny responsibility for my own actions and attitudes by blaming others?

Sometimes, the holiness of another stuns me. I never expected to see grace shining through the eyes of that person. I never imagined that someone I might consider insignificant or even despicable could teach me about love or forgiveness.

C. GIVE HEART TO COURAGE

Many times during his long life, Tagore publicly endorsed, or opposed, something that shone an uncomfortable spotlight on him. Those situations included: opposing Gandhi on many issues;[121] accepting gifts and hospitality from Mussolini and then later apologizing for his prior ignorance about the dictator's tyranny; and chal-lenging several world leaders to recognize the dangers of patriotism at the expense of the greater humanity.[122] Despite his pain, Tagore responded with courage to situations he thought were unjust or misunderstood.

Grief can paralyze us into a state of numbness or inactivity. Feelings of helplessness can be just as destructive as whatever the precipitating event might be. The root of the word "courage" means "heart." Rather than allowing a situation to break one's heart, courage calls us to respond from the heart. This is not to minimize or ignore the feelings of grief. Sometimes, people refuse to give the grief a place in their lives. This pretense that all is well grows into a poison, manifesting in the denial of other feelings and relationships. How much time one needs to hold the grief, and what one does with it, is subjective. No formulas or timetables can accurately map the grief process. The balance between feeling the grief in a healthy way, and channeling it into another activity, varies as much as life itself.

One of our most revered and courageous leaders, Dr. Martin Luther King, Jr. responded to racial oppression and violence based on the teachings and example of Mohandas Gandhi. Everyone recognizes that the actions of both men exemplified tremendous courage. What people may not realize is that Tagore feared and predicted correctly that Gandhi's initial anti-British stance would devolve into violence.[123] So many times, throughout the world's history, violence preceded peaceful resistance.

By 1919, when Tagore publicly denounced the British-led police state that enabled and commended violence against non-British Indians, the poet's reputation and fame were legendary.[124] How easy it would have been for him to shake his head in despair, send some rupees to some affiliated helping organization, and return to his work. In a letter to the viceroy, Lord Chelmsford, which quickly received significant publicity, Tagore lamented how a recent legislation diminished ordinary Indian citizens. Like Dr. King and Gandhi, Tagore displayed courage in protesting persons and events that he considered wrong-hearted, while he grieved what was happening and how his responses were received.

For most of us, acting courageously during a season of grief will not be as dramatic or public as Tagore's actions. The most courageous activity I might be able to summon could be to attend a public event with a friend, or to ask a neighbor for help. Acknowledging within myself that it took courage, and that I succeeded in that small action shall inch me towards healing. How much healthier that mindset is than considering myself weak and needy.

In the moment when a grieving person acts courageously, one may not suspect any hope of healing from that action. Later, though, the strength of that pursuit cloaks one with resolve and hope, like the dawn of a new morning.

D. DELIGHT IN NATURE

Despite that our home is only minutes away from several major interstate highways, our little neighborhood is as peaceful as they come.

Our property and all the properties in our neighborhood sit right on the edge of county parkland, so we are surrounded by woods that will never be destroyed for suburbia. I am grateful for this slice of heaven. The trees, the rippling creek, the multitude of birds, squirrels, deer, raccoons, and foxes bless me every day.

Tagore's poems overflow with references to nature, to the seasons of the year, types of trees and flowers, and to the swimming, flying, walking, and crawling creatures. He often recounts how therapeutic and necessary it is for him to breathe and observe and embrace the natural world.

Uncle Sam sent me to South Korea from the spring of 1988 until the spring of 1989. Spring in South Korea resembles stepping into a Monet painting. Flowers and shrubs and trees reflect colors of every hue. The florid greens of the grass and the blinding yellows of the mustard fields seem almost psychedelic. The beauty contrasts with how crowded and overdeveloped the little country is. The parks I visited provided a welcomed and popular oasis of healing and joy for me and millions of others.

I had a similar experience in India. I delighted in the exquisite flowers thriving on the grounds of the ashram where I stayed. The vivid colors and sounds of various species of birds never ceased to amaze me. As in Korea, the Indian villages and cities clogged my senses with exhaust fumes, garbage, and ceaseless noise. And always, I worried that whatever vehicle I was in might strike a stray dog, a goat, a cow, a cyclist, or a pedestrian.

Tagore hated living and traveling in big cities, but he couldn't accomplish all that he needed to do from the cocoon of his ashram school in the country, so he ventured out into the populous frenzy for long periods over and over. He felt whole again when he could commune with nature.[125]

Many of us in the United States have easy access to areas of nature. So much healing energy invites us into the natural world. Tagore's prayer professes his gratitude for the aspects of nature.

> If you did not fill my heart with love
> Why then have you suffused the morning skies with such songs? Why have you strung garlands from stars and made a bed out of flowers?
> Why does the spring breeze whisper sweet nothings into my ears? If you did not fill my heart with love
> Why does the sky gaze so soulfully at my countenance?
>
> —Tagore[126]

E. CREATIVE ARTS

Whatever creative activity that calls to you will strengthen your life and help heal your grief. That may be gardening, cooking, repairing something, working with children, or decorating someone's home—the list is endless. The emotions one experiences during a season of grief frequently race up and down like a roller coaster. Summoning energy and concentration may seem like the impossible dream, so intentionally setting a time and place to do something you enjoy offers a respite. If you can't manage to "do" anything, then just listen to a song or a poem, gaze at beautiful artwork, or sit in a park or a garden.

When I studied how to offer healing music to people who are sick or dying, I learned to match that person's mood or breathing. It's called entrainment, and it refers to resonating with the other person. We need to do that for ourselves sometimes, to honor and reflect what is going on inside. Singing and dancing, for example, are therapeutic when the mood and tempo are slow, and reflective when I'm feeling slow and reflective. Engaging in some sort of creative activity is not the point. The point is to honor whatever emotion needs recognition at that time.

During his most difficult times, Tagore's poems and his paintings became his therapy. So plant some flowers, volunteer at the animal shelter, bake some cookies, or write a poem. For a few moments, the pain and chaos may subside. That little respite will do you good.

F. EMBRACE THE DIVINE FEMININE

"My eternal sorrow will be my eternal treasure."[127]

We don't equate sorrow and treasure. We have become so accustomed to fearing sorrow, to think of it as something to be shunned. Yet many of the world's greatest events arose because of some great sorrow.

They say that necessity is the mother of invention. I think that adage is backwards. Mother is the necessity who pushes us to new realms of invention and creativity. Mother Earth, Mother Nature,

Mother Mary, Mother Ganga, Mother Shakti help us turn inward to our feminine natures for hope and comfort and inspiration when we feel frightened or discouraged or lonely.

The feminine aspects of ourselves and of Divinity reflect our highest selves. When we allow ourselves to embrace the "gift of sorrow," we can more fully share compassion with all life. When we treasure sorrow and joy, we become whole. Tagore did not teach the illusoriness of sorrow, nor the avoidance of sorrow. He taught and lived that sorrow is our greatest teacher. Embracing the Divine Feminine gives us the courage to embrace the pain and sorrow and find ways to birth them into life-giving energy, invention, inspiration, and insight.

G. *INTENTIONAL SPACE FOR QUIET LISTENING, & BEING, NOT DOING*

Don't just do something. Sit there. Breathe. Listen to your heart. Embrace the stillness.

[119] Tagore, 2008b, #44, p. 288
[120] Tagore, in Som, 2009, p. 242
[121] Das Gupta, 2013, pp. 103–113
[122] Das Gupta, 2013, pp. 117–24
[123] Dutta & Robinson, Eds., 2005, pp. 236–7
[124] Dutta & Robinson, 2005, pp. 222–5
[125] Das Gupta, 2006, pp. 165–7
[126] Tagore, in Som, 2009, p. 259
[127] Tagore, 2008b, # 135, p. 243

The Journey Continues

My husband Wayne left this earthly life on Friday afternoon, July 25, 2014. He died in our home, surrounded by me, our two cats, and our old coonhound. All of us were broken for a very long time.

I believe that the spirit of Tagore has been guiding and encouraging me for almost twenty years. I have learned much from him and look forward to continuing that process.

The definition of grief that I proposed at the beginning of this book remains as constant as the sunrise: grief is whenever someone or something you love, cherish, or prize is lost, stolen, or dies. And what have I learned about myself through all of this? When I'm in the midst of something that torments me, I am not as strong or independent as I want to be, or as other people think I am. In fact, I feel quite vulnerable and needy during those times. I don't think that's a bad thing. The prevalent messages about grief in our society focus on staying strong and not "losing it." Neither comforting nor healing, those messages diminish the opportunity for honest sorrow and healing.

In 1993, six weeks after my former husband Jerry died, I asked the senior chaplain if I could preach a farewell sermon to the military congregation I had helped pastor for three years. Despite having barely been able to do anything except weep since Jerry's funeral, I needed to stand in front of those folks and tell them how much I loved them and try to offer some spiritual sustenance one more time. The dear ones in that chapel congregation knew that I was moving from Oklahoma to northern Virginia within the week, and we shared many tears. One of the retirees, whose army career had included World War II and the Korean War, told me that my sermon that

Sunday was one of the bravest things he had ever witnessed. I did not understand what he meant, but I never forgot it. I understand now: grieving is soul-wrenching, and it is difficult in our grief- denying culture to expose oneself that nakedly. I could never have risked that had I not been positive that I was surrounded by love and prayers. We must take great and gentle care of ourselves when we grieve.

Tagore has taught me much about healthy grieving. The path to wholeness is what he never tired of saying, no matter the circumstance or the culture. He didn't limit his recipe to grief situations. It is the secret for the world: we need each other. When we live that truth, we are likely to see God.

> Guests of my life,
> You came in the early dawn, and you in the night,
> Your name was uttered by the Spring flowers and yours by the showers of rain.
> You brought the harp into my house and you brought the lamp. After you had taken your leave I found God's footprints on my floor.
> Now when I am at the end of my pilgrimage I leave in the evening flowers of worship my salutations to you all.
> —Tagore[128]

[128] Tagore, 2011a, "Crossing," #75, p. 239

Linda L. George, Ph.D.

References

American Psychological Association. (2009). *Publication manual of the American Psychological Association (6th ed.)*. Washington, DC: Author.

Arnold, D., & Blackburn, S. (Eds.). (2004). *Telling lives in India: Biography, autobiography, and life history*. Bloomington, IN: IN University.

Aurobindo, S. (1995). *The foundations of Indian culture*. Pondicherry, India: Sri Aurobindo Ashram. (Original work published serially 1918– 1921)

Bailey, K. E. (2008). *Jesus through middle Eastern eyes: Cultural studies in the gospels*. Downers Grove, L: InterVarsity.

Barone, T., & Eisner, E. W. (2012). *Arts based research*. Thousand Oaks, CA: Sage.

Basham, A. L. (Ed.). (2012). *A cultural history of India*. New Delhi: Oxford University. (Original work published 1975)

Basu, T. K. (2005). *Village life in Bengal*. R. Stevenson (Ed.). NY: iUniverse. (Original work entitled The Bengal peasant from time to time, published 1962)

Bhattacharya, S. (2011). *Rabindranath Tagore: An interpretation*. Delhi: Penguin Group.

Bhattacharya, S. (Ed.). (1999). *The Mahatma and the poet: Letters and debates between Gandhi and Tagore 1915-1941*. New Delhi: National Book Trust. (Original work published 1921)

Biklen, S. K., & Casella, R. (2007). *A practical guide to the qualitative dissertation*. NY: Teachers College, Columbia University.

Bloomberg, L. D., & Volpe, M. (2008). *Completing your qualitative dissertation: A roadmap from beginning to end*. Los Angeles: Sage.

Boring, M. E., & Craddock, F. B. (2004). *The people's New Testament commentary*. Louisville, KY: Westminster John Knox.

Bose, B. C. (2005). *Hindu customs in Bengal*. R. Stevenson (Ed.). NY: iUniverse. (Original work written 1875, n.d. original publication)

Brown, B. (2012). *Daring Greatly: How the courage to be vulnerable transforms the way we live, love, parent, and lead*. NY: Gotham Books.

Cain, S. (2012). *Quiet: The power of introverts in a world that can't stop talking*. NY: Crown.

Campbell, J. (2003). *Myths of light: Eastern metaphors of the eternal*. D. Kudler (Ed.). Novato, CA: New World Library.

Chilton, B. (2002). *Rabbi Jesus: An intimate biography*. NY: Image Books.

Clothey, F. (2006). *Religion in India: A historical introduction*. NY: Routledge.

Das Gupta, U. (Ed.). (2003). *A difficult friendship: Letters of Edward Thompson and Rabindranath Tagore*. New Delhi: Oxford University.

Das Gupta, U. (2004). *Rabindranath Tagore: A biography*. New Delhi: Oxford University.

Das Gupta, U. (2013). *Rabindranath Tagore: An illustrated life*. New Delhi: Oxford University.

Deb, C. (2010). *Women of the Tagore household*. (S. Chowdhry & S. Roy, Trans.). NY: Penguin Group.

Denzin, N. K. (1989). *Interpretive biography*. (Qualitative research methods series 17). Newbury Park, CA: Sage.

Didion, J. (2007). *The year of magical thinking*. NY: Vintage International.

Didion, J. (2011). *Blue nights*. NY: Alfred A. Knopf.

Doniger, W. (2009). *The Hindus: An alternative history*. NY: Penguin Press.

Dutta, K., & Robinson, A. (Eds.). (2005). *Selected letters of Rabindranath Tagore*. (Foreword by A. Sen.). New Delhi: Cambridge University.

Dutta, K., & Robinson, A. (2009). *Rabindranath Tagore: The myriad- minded man.* London: Bloomsbury. (Original work published 1995)

Eck, D. (1998). *Darśan: Seeing the divine image in India (3rd Ed.).* NY: Columbia University.

Flood, G. (1996). *An introduction to Hinduism.* NY: Cambridge University.

Foss, S. K., & Waters, W. (2007). *Destination dissertation: A traveler's guide to a done dissertation.* NY: Rowman & Littlefield.

Friedrichs, K. (1986). Gayatri. In Schumacher, S. & Woerner, G. (Eds.), *The encyclopedia of eastern philosophy and religion: Buddhism, Hinduism, Taoism, Zen.* Boston: Shambala.

Friedrichs, K. (1986). Vedas. In Schumacher, S. & Woerner, G. (Eds.), *The encyclopedia of eastern philosophy and religion: Buddhism, Hinduism, Taoism, Zen.* Boston: Shambala.

Ghose, S. (1989). *The late poems of Tagore.* New Delhi: Sterling. (original work published 1961)

Golden, T. R. (2000). *Swallowed by a snake: The gift of the masculine side of healing (2nd ed.).* Gaithersburg, MD: Golden Healing. (Original work published 1996)

Greenspan, M. (2004). *Healing through the dark emotions: The wisdom of grief, fear, and despair.* Boston: Shambhala.

Heehs, P. (Ed.). *Indian religions: A historical reader of spiritual expression and experience.* Washington Square, NY: NY University Press.

Holroyde, P. (2007). *An ABC of Indian culture: A personal padayatra of half a century into India.* Ocean Township, NJ: Grantha Corp.

James, J. W., & Friedman, R. (2009). *The grief recovery handbook: The action program for moving beyond death, divorce, and other losses including health, career, and faith* (20th anniversary expanded ed.). NY: Harper-Collins. (Original work published 1988)

Kopf, D. (2011). *The Brahmo samaj and the shaping of the modern Indian mind.* New Delhi: Atlantic.

Kripalani, K. (2008). *Rabindranath Tagore: A biography.* (Revised ed.). Calcutta: Visva-Bharati. (Original work published 1962)

Kubler-Ross, E. and Kessler, D. (2005). *On grief and grieving: Finding the meaning of grief through the five stages of loss.* NY: Scribner.

Lago, M. M. (Ed.). (1972). *Imperfect encounter: Letters of William Rothenstein and Rabindranath Tagore, 1911-1941.* New Delhi: National Book Trust.

Lago, M. M. (1976). *Rabindranath Tagore.* Boston: G. K. Hall.

Lewis, C. S. (1976). *A grief observed.* NY: Bantam Books. (Original work published 1963)

Machi, L. A., & McEvoy, B. T. (2009). *The literature review.* Thousand Oaks, CA: Corwin.

Mansingh, S. (2000). *Historical dictionary of India.* New Delhi: Vision Books. (Original work published 1998)

Martin, C. R. (1997). *Looking at type: The fundamentals.* Gainesville, FL: Center for Applications of Psychological Type.

Mines, D. P., & Lamb, S. (Eds.). (2010). *Everyday life in south Asia (2nd Ed.).* Bloomington, IN: IN University.

Moustakas, C. (1990). *Heuristic research: Design, methodology, and applications.* Newbury Park, CA: Sage.

Pandey, G. (2013). *A history of prejudice: Race, caste, and difference in India and the United States.* NY: Cambridge University.

Pearson, W. W. (2010). *Shantiniketan: The Bolpur school of Rabindranath Tagore.* London: Macmillan. (Original work published 1916)

Reissman, C. K. (1993). *Narrative analysis.* (Qualitative research methods series 30). Newbury Park, CA: Sage.

Rhys, E. (n. d. of reproduction). *Rabindranath Tagore: A biographical study.* New York: Macmillan. (Original work published 1916)

Sarkar, S. (2010). *The Swadeshi movement in Bengal, 1903–1908 (2nd Ed.).* New Delhi: Sapra Brothers. (Original work published 1973)

Seager, R. H. (2009). *The world's parliament of religions: The East/West encounter, Chicago, 1893.* Bloomington, IN: IN University.

Sharma, S. R. (2003). *Life and works of Rabindranath Tagore.* Jaipur, India: Book Enclave.

Som, R. (2009). *Rabindranath Tagore: The singer and his song.* New Delhi: Penguin Books.

Tagore, D. (n. d. of reproduction). *The autobiography of Maharshi Devendranath Tagore*. (S. Tagore, & I. Devi, Trans.). Calcutta: S. K. Lahiri. (Original work published 1909)

Tagore, R. (1921). *Glimpses of Bengal: Selected from the letters of Sir Rabindranath Tagore, 1885 to 1895*. Rockville, MD: Arc Manor. (Original work published 1920)

Tagore, R. (1995). *I won't let you go: Selected poems*. (K. K. Dyson, Trans.). New Delhi: UBS. (Original work published 1992)

Tagore, R. (1997a). *Gitanjali: A collection of prose translations made by the author from the original Bengali*. (With intro. by W. B. Yeats). London: Macmillan. (Original work published 1913)

Tagore, R. (1997b). *The heart of God: Prayers of Rabindranath Tagore*. H. F. Vetter (Ed.). Boston: Charles E. Tuttle.

Tagore, R. (2001). *Rabindranath Tagore: Final poems*. (W. Barker, & S. Tagore, Trans.). NY: George Braziller.

Tagore, R. (2002a). *Letters to a friend: Rabindranath Tagore's letters to C.F. Andrews*. C. F. Andrews (Ed.). New Delhi: Rupa. (Original work published 1928)

Tagore, R. (2002b). *Show yourself to my soul: A new translation of Gitanjali*. (J. Talarovic, Trans.). Bangladesh: University Press. (Original work published 1983)

Tagore, R. (2004a). *The art of Tagore*. New Delhi: Rupa & Co.

Tagore, R. (2004b). *Sadhana: The realization of life*. London: Doubleday. (Original work published 1913)

Tagore, R. (2005a). *Lipika: Prose poems*. (A. Bose, Trans.). New Delhi: Rupa & Co.

Tagore, R. (2005b). *Selected poems*. (W. Radice, Trans.). London: Penguin Books. (Original work published 1985)

Tagore, R. (2006). *My life in my words*. Uma Das Gupta (Ed.). New Delhi: Penguin Books.

Tagore, R. (2008a). *Glimpses of Bengal: Selected from the letters of Rabindranath Tagore, 1885-1895*. Rockville, MD: Arc Manor.

Tagore, R. (2008b). *Of love, nature, and devotion: Selected songs of Rabindranath Tagore*. (K. Bardhan, Trans.). New Delhi: Oxford University.

Tagore, R. (2011a). *The English writings of Rabindranath Tagore, Vol. 1: Poems*. Das, S. K. (Ed.) Delhi:Sahitya Akademi.

Tagore, R. (2011b). *The essential Tagore*. Alam F., & Chakravarty, A. (Eds.) Cambridge, MA: Belknap.

Tagore, R. (2011c). *Gitanjali: song offerings*. (W. Radice, Trans.). New Delhi: Penguin Books.

Tagore, R. [Rathindranath]. (1981). *On the edges of time*. Calcutta: Visva- Bharati. (Original work published 1958)

Thompson, E. (1992). *Rabindranath Tagore: Poet and dramatist*. Delhi: Oxford University. (Original work published 1948)

Webster's ninth new collegiate dictionary. (1988). Springfield, MA: Merriam-Webster.

Zimmer, H. (1961). *Philosophies of India*. J. Campbell (Ed.). NY: World Publishing. (Original work published 1951)

Zimmer, H. (1972). *Myths and symbols in Indian art and civilization*. (Bollingen series 6). Joseph Campbell (Ed.). Princeton, NJ: Princeton University.

www.ingramcontent.com/pod-product-compliance
Lightning Source LLC
LaVergne TN
LVHW010217070526
838199LV00062B/4634